KU-790-376

WITHDRAWN

Competing Values Leadership

NEWMAN UNIVERSITY
COLLEGE
BARTLEY GREEN
BIRMINGHAM B32 3NT

CLASS 658. 4092

BARCODE 01632353

AUTHOR CAM

NEW HORIZONS IN MANAGEMENT

Series Editor: Cary L. Cooper, *CBE, Professor of Organizational Psychology and Health, Lancaster University Management School, Lancaster University, UK.*

This important series makes a significant contribution to the development of management thought. This field has expanded dramatically in recent years and the series provides an invaluable forum for the publication of high quality work in management science, human resource management, organizational behaviour, marketing, management information systems, operations management, business ethics, strategic management and international management.

The main emphasis of the series is on the development and application of new original ideas. International in its approach, it will include some of the best theoretical and empirical work from both well-established researchers and the new generation of scholars.

Competing Values Leadership

Creating Value in Organizations

Kim S. Cameron, Robert E. Quinn and Jeff DeGraff

University of Michigan, Ann Arbor, USA

and

Anjan V. Thakor

Washington University, USA

NEW HORIZONS IN MANAGEMENT

Edward Elgar
Cheltenham, UK • Northampton, MA, USA

© Kim S. Cameron, Robert E. Quinn, Jeff DeGraff, Anjan V. Thakor, 2006

All rights reserved. No part of this publication may be reproduced, stored in a retrieval system or transmitted in any form or by any means, electronic, mechanical or photocopying, recording, or otherwise without the prior permission of the publisher.

Published by
Edward Elgar Publishing Limited
Glensanda House
Montpellier Parade
Cheltenham
Glos GL50 1UA
UK

Edward Elgar Publishing, Inc.
136 West Street
Suite 202
Northampton
Massachusetts 01060
USA

A catalogue record for this book
is available from the British Library

Library of Congress Cataloguing-in-Publication Data
Competing values leadership : creating value in organizations / Kim S. Cameron . . . [et al.].
      p. cm.
Includes bibliographical references and index.
1. Leadership. 2. Organizational change. 3. Corporate culture. 4. Organizational behavior.   I. Cameron, Kim S.

HD57.7.C646 2006
658.4′092–dc22
                                                                        2005054875

ISBN-13: 978 1 84542 735 1 (cased)
ISBN-10: 1 84542 735 1 (cased)

Printed and bound in Great Britain by the MPG Books Group

Contents

Figures

Tables

PART I

Value creation

1. Introducing the competing values way of thinking

Ralph Waldo Emerson (1850) declared: 'It is the last lesson of modern science, that the highest simplicity of structure is produced, not by few elements, but by the highest complexity.'

This statement suggests that simplicity and complexity can often be confused with one another. In the case of novices, for example, a superficial or cursory understanding of something leads to a simple explanation. Simplicity in this sense results from lack of awareness, naivety, or underappreciation. Explanations are simple because complexity is ignored, and such explanations tend to have limited application and value.

Experts, on the other hand, are cognizant of the complexity of a phenomenon and, therefore, are aware of the multiple and complicated elements. Their explanations tend to be characterized as elaborate and intricate. They demonstrate a much greater degree of understanding than the novice. It is often difficult to capture their understanding or meaning, however, because their explanations are more complicated and convoluted than those of the novice. Experts can convey the complexity of things, but not in simple terms.

Masters understand in much greater depth and detail what novices and experts observe, but their explanations also have much more value and application. They organize complexity into profoundly simple terms. Their explanations represent what Emerson described – the simplicity that lies at the heart of complexity. They understand the phenomenon so completely that they are able to explain complicated things in simple terms. The difference between the simplicity of novices and the simplicity of masters lies not in the surface presentation but in the profound depth of understanding that lies beneath it.

We pay masters many times more that we pay experts. When we approach masters for explanations, we tend to be profoundly influenced by what they say – not because it is more complex but because it is profoundly simpler. Masters share the simple structure embedded within complexity.

VALUE

Creating value is an enormously complex endeavor both for leaders and for organizations. Yet, despite its complexity, value creation is the objective of every enterprise, every worker, and every leader. All employees are judged by their ability to create value. Traditionally, value creation is defined in terms of financial measures – profitability, revenue increases, or cost savings. Considering only the financial part of value creation, however, is similar to the simplicity of the novice. It is accurate but incomplete. Experienced executives know that value creation represents much more complexity than straightforwardly measured financial indicators.

Experienced executives adopt a more complex view. They may, for example, speak of the need to assess 'intangible' assets as well as 'tangible' assets, and to consider value creation in a 'balanced scorecard' kind of way. They recognize that a variety of indicators are associated with value creation, but the diversity and complexity of these indicators make them difficult to understand and communicate. The simple structure underlying value creation is obscured by an awareness of the complexity that is associated with it.

In this book, we attempt to represent the role of a master. That is, we try to convey the profound simplicity associated with value creation. We show that there is a profoundly simple underlying framework that can identify the factors that produce the most value in individuals and organizations. To understand this underlying structure is to begin to grasp the highest levels of complexity in ways that can be useful and practical.

We explain a framework that can help leaders understand more deeply and act more effectively in creating value. This framework – The Competing Values Framework – helps leaders see, in the tensions of organizational life, levels of potential that others do not. Leaders can become more like masters in that they can detect ways to create value in unexpected ways. This ability to see the profound simplicity in complexity is the essence of mastery.

In short, this book is intended to help leaders discover the structure of value by becoming familiar with the Competing Values Framework, its implications, and its practices. In order to do this the book is divided into two parts. In the first five chapters, we discuss the core elements of the Competing Values Framework and focus on rethinking the notion of value. In the next four chapters we emphasize specific tools and techniques leaders can use to make sustainable change.

In Chapters 2 through 5 we show how the dimensions of the Competing Values Framework help leaders expand their leadership repertoire and broaden their definitions of value. Because everyone has a tendency to pay attention to certain phenomena more than others – for example, central figures get more attention than background in photographs – we provide tools and techniques that help leaders learn to broaden their thinking in ways that lead to more creativity, understand more complexity, and create more value.

In Chapters 6 through 9 we offer three methods for leading change and creating value. The first method uses financial measures to show how organizations can markedly enhance financial value and shareholder wealth, and it explains how the Competing Values Framework can be used to predict stock price. Using this information, it is possible to build a change strategy informed by more rigorous economic arguments. Economic data from major corporations are used to illustrate this process.

A second method builds on the first and derives from 25 years of research and intervention in major organizations (Cameron and Quinn, 2006). It identifies the cultural and organizational competencies that give rise to value creation. It explains how cultural and leadership competencies can be profiled which, in turn, can lead to a diagnosis of culture gaps, cultural congruence, and cultural strength. Techniques for culture change are explained. The discussion also shows how this kind of culture and management analysis can be used to accurately predict the success of mergers and acquisitions.

The third method identifies some daily practices that help foster the leadership, cultural, and organizational competencies that produce a desired financial outcome. It provides basic levers that are readily accessible to leaders which can enhance individual and organizational performance and foster the creation of value.

In short, the book provides a language of value creation, a simple structure of value, and a set of techniques and practices for enhancing value. The underlying Competing Values Framework helps leaders think differently about value creation and shows them how to clarify purpose, integrate practices, and lead people.

THE COMPETING VALUES FRAMEWORK

The Competing Values Framework has been named as one of the 40 most important frameworks in the history of business (ten Have et al., 2003). It has been studied and tested in organizations for more than 25 years by a group of thought leaders from leading business schools and corporations (Quinn and Cameron, 1983; Quinn and Rohrbaugh, 1983; Quinn, 1988; Cameron and Quinn, 2006). Currently used by hundreds of firms around the world, the Competing Values Framework emerged from studies of the factors that account for highly effective organizational performance. It was

Figure 1.1   The relationship between leadership, effective performance, and value creation

developed in response to the need for a broadly applicable model that would foster successful leadership, improve organizational effectiveness, and promote value creation (see Figure 1.1).

The Competing Values Framework serves as a map, an organizing mechanism, a sense-making device, a source of new ideas, and a learning system. It has been applied by researchers and practitioners to many aspects of organizations such as value outcomes, corporate strategy, organizational culture, core competencies, leadership, communication, decision making, motivation, human resources practices, quality, and employee selection (see Cameron and Quinn, 2006). From the Competing Values Framework comes a theory about how these various aspects of organizations function in simultaneous harmony and tension with one another. The framework helps identify a set of guidelines that can enable leaders to diagnose and manage the interrelationships, congruencies, and contradictions among these different aspects of organizations. In other words, the framework helps leaders work more comprehensively and more consistently in improving their organizations' performance and value creation.

More than two decades of work on the Competing Values Framework has produced a set of intervention processes, measurement devices, and change techniques that capture a comprehensive view of the organization, its outcomes, and its leadership. As we explain below, the framework highlights the inherent tensions and contradictions that face organizations and leaders as they navigate their complex and changing environments. It predicts the future success of enterprises with significantly greater accuracy than alternative models currently on the market. It goes beyond the capabilities of other approaches to leadership development, organizational change, or financial valuation in its ability to forecast, measure, and create positive value in organizations.

CORE DIMENSIONS

As mentioned previously, statistical analyses have confirmed the robustness and applicability of this framework to a broad array of human and organizational phenomena. That is, the same dimensions that emerged from research on organizational effectiveness also emerged when studying a wide variety of other aspects of human and organizational activities, including shareholder value, mergers and acquisitions, approaches to learning, organizational culture, leadership competencies, organizational designs, communication styles, organizational virtues, creativity, financial investments, and information processing. The underlying dimensions that organize each of these various phenomena are not only consistent, they can be illustrated as in Figure 1.2.

All organized human activity has an underlying structure. Completely haphazard actions, or randomly dispersed elements, for example, are said to be without organization. Hence, organization, by definition, connotes patterns and predictability in relationships. Identifying the underlying dimensions of organization that exist in almost all human and organizational activity is one of the key functions of the Competing Values Framework. It helps uncover the underlying relationships that reside in

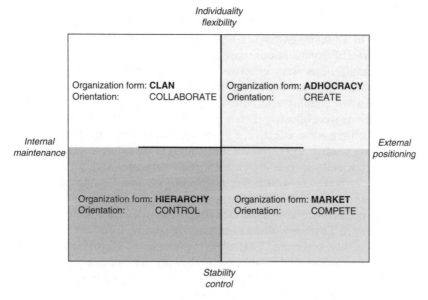

Figure 1.2   Core dimensions of the Competing Values Framework

organizations, leadership, learning, culture, motivation, decision making, cognitive processing, creativity, and so on.

Other writers have made similar claims – that a universal underlying structure can be identified. Two recent ones are colleagues Paul Lawrence and Nitin Noria (2002), who identified the four biologically determined drives located in the brain that, they claim, account for virtually all human behavior – drives to bond, to learn, to acquire, and to defend. These four motivations replicate precisely the dimensions of the Competing Values Framework, and the drives can be categorized exactly in the four quadrants in the framework. A second is philosopher Ken Wilber (2001) who asserted in his book – modestly entitled, *A Theory of Everything* – that the universe can be explained on the basis of a single framework, represented in four quadrants – social systems, organic brain activity, culture and worldliness, and self-consciousness. Again, Wilber's framework reproduces precisely the dimensions of the Competing Values Framework.

Unlike Lawrence, Noria, and Wilber, we do not claim to have developed a universal theory of everything, nor do we claim to explain all human motivation and action, but we do maintain that the Competing Values Framework can be useful to almost all leaders. It can help them understand the simple structure that underlies all organizing activities. It can also help them create new and more effective patterns of organizing.

The basic framework consists of two dimensions that express the tensions or 'competing values' that exist in all organizations. Graphically, one dimension can be drawn vertically and the other drawn horizontally – resulting in a two-by-two figure with four quadrants. When studying the effectiveness of organizations more than two decades ago, we noticed that some organizations were effective if they demonstrated flexibility and adaptability, but other organizations were effective if they demonstrated the opposite – stability and control. Similarly, we discovered that some organizations were effective if they maintained efficient internal processes whereas others were effective if they maintained competitive external positioning relative to customers and clients. These differences represent the different ends of two dimensions, each with opposing anchors, and these dimensions constitute the rudiments of the Competing Values Framework.

More specifically, one dimension of the framework differentiates an orientation toward flexibility, discretion, and dynamism from an orientation toward stability, order, and control. For example, on the one hand, some organizations are viewed as effective if they are changing, adaptable, and organic – for instance, neither the product mix nor the organizational form stays in place very long at firms such as Microsoft or Nike – since agility and volatility typify their performance and are keys to their success.

Other organizations are viewed as effective if they are stable, predictable, and mechanistic – for instance, most universities, government agencies, and organizations such as the New York Stock Exchange, Coca-Cola, and Anheuser-Busch are characterized by longevity and steadiness in both design and output – so performance is consistent and even.

One dimension of the Competing Values Framework, in other words, represents a continuum ranging from versatility and pliability on one end to consistency and durability on the other end. When referring to individuals, this dimension differentiates people who learn inductively, communicate with animated and speculative ideas, and process information by searching for innovative applications, on the one hand, compared to people who learn deductively, communicate with rational and considered ideas, and process information methodically, on the other hand (Lawrence and Noria, 2002).

The second dimension of the framework differentiates an orientation toward a focus on internal capability and the integration and unity of processes on the one hand, from an orientation toward a focus on external opportunities and differentiation from and rivalry with outsiders on the other hand. That is, some organizations produce value associated with their harmonious internal characteristics – for instance, Dell and Hewlett-Packard have traditionally been recognized for a consistent 'Dell-way' or 'H-P way.' Other organizations produce value primarily by focusing on challenging and competing with rivals outside their boundaries – for instance, Toyota and Honda are known for 'thinking globally but acting locally' when competing with American car companies, or for encouraging units to adopt the attributes of local environments instead of a centrally prescribed approach.

This dimension ranges, in other words, from cohesion and consonance on the one end to separation and independence on the other. When referring to individuals, this dimension differentiates people who learn by examining familiar information, communicate using harmonizing strategies, and processing information by analysing consistencies and congruencies on the one hand, from people who learn by searching for unfamiliar elements, communicate using confronting strategies, and process information by analysing uniquenesses, aberrations, and dissimilarities on the other hand.

In order to create value in organizations, it is sometimes effective to focus on expanding options, creating new ideas, self-organizing, and collaborative learning (i.e., focusing on the Collaborate and Create quadrants in Figure 1.2). Coping successfully with the changing conditions of twenty-first century environments, for example, requires constant adaptability and flexibility. The half-life of almost any technology on the planet is less than six months, so conservative thinkers and laggards in new product development will most certainly be left behind – just ask leaders in 3M, Microsoft, or Amazon.com.

Other times value is best pursued by focusing on maintaining objectivity, gathering and analysing data, and carefully monitoring progress (i.e., focusing on the Control and Compete quadrants in Figure 1.2). Just as constant change requires the identification of something stable to be effectively managed (Cameron, 2006), so also organizations require predictability and reliability to produce lasting value. Companies that consistently outperform the market over time are those that have stable cultures, consistent visions, and dependable processes, including firms such as Harley-Davidson, Rubbermaid, and Walgreens (Collins and Porras, 1994).

Creating value also can be pursued by focusing on external opportunities such as acquisitions, identifying future trends, pursuing innovative ideas, and competing for market share and growth (the Create and Compete quadrants in Figure 1.2). The focus is on the right side of the framework, or on opportunities located outside the boundaries of the organization. General Electric, for example, has remained one of the world's most successful firms by constantly engaging, acquiring, and competing with entities outside its the traditional market niches (Tichy and Sherman, 2001).

On the other hand, value creation may also occur through an emphasis on internal capability, or on systems, culture, cost reduction, continuous quality improvement, and human development (the Collaborate and Control quadrants in Figure 1.2). The focus is on the left side of the framework, or on elements located inside organizational boundaries. General Electric is also a good example of a company that created enormous value by adopting an internal six-sigma quality initiative (that is, an emphasis on a dramatic reduction in errors) implementing a massive efficiency-producing program called 'workout,' and fostered a wholesale adoption of the Internet as a way of doing business.

Together these two core dimensions form four quadrants, each representing a distinct cluster of criteria – whether referring to leadership, effectiveness, value creation, structure, learning, or other organizationally-relevant factors. The resulting framework represents the way people evaluate organizations, the way they process information and learn about their environments, the way they organize and lead others, the kinds of value created for customers, the clustering of organizational elements, and what people see as good, right, and appropriate. It captures the fundamental values – or culture – that exist in organizations (Cameron and Quinn, 2006). Most important, for our purposes, it identifies the multiple ways in which value can be created and measured in organizations.

What is notable about these four quadrants is that they represent opposite or competing assumptions. Each continuum highlights value creation and key performance criteria that are opposite from the value creation and performance criteria on the other end of the continuum – i.e., flexibility versus stability, internal focus versus external focus. The dimensions, therefore, produce quadrants that are also contradictory or competing on the diagonal.

The upper left quadrant in Figure 1.2, for example, identifies value creation and performance criteria that emphasize an internal, organic focus, whereas the lower right quadrant identifies value creation and performance criteria that emphasize an external, control focus. Similarly, the upper right quadrant identifies value creation and performance criteria that emphasize an external, organic focus whereas the lower left quadrant emphasizes internal, control value creation and performance criteria. These competing or opposite elements in each quadrant give rise to one of the most important features of the Competing Values Framework, the presence and necessity of paradox.

Each of the four quadrants has been given a label in order to characterize its most notable characteristics for creating value. The original formulation of the Competing Vales Framework used terms derived from the scholarly literature in organizational studies to define each quadrant – Clan (upper left), Adhocracy (upper right), Market (lower right), and Hierarchy (lower left) (Cameron and Quinn, 2006). In communicating to practicing leaders and managers, however, we have found it helpful to substitute action verbs as labels which can cue leaders as to the kinds of dominant activities that relate to value creation in each quadrant – Collaborate, Create, Compete, and Control. We will use the latter verbs through this book.

As noted in Figure 1.2, the Collaborate quadrant is at the upper left, the Create quadrant is at the upper right, the Compete quadrant is at the lower right, and the Control quadrant is at the lower left. The two upper quadrants share an emphasis on flexibility and dynamism, whereas the two bottom quadrants share an emphasis on stability and control. The two left-hand quadrants focus on internal capability whereas the two right-hand quadrants focus on external opportunity. What is important to remember is that the quadrants represent clusters of similar elements and similar orientations, but those elements and orientations are contradictory to those in the diagonal quadrant. The dimensions in the framework, in other words, separate opposite, competing, or paradoxical elements on the diagonal.

COLORS

In teaching the framework we have often found it useful to rely on colors to identify the quadrants. On the cover of this book, for example, a colored version of the framework is displayed. The Collaborate quadrant is yellow, the Create quadrant is green, the Compete quadrant is blue, and the Control quadrant is red. People frequently find it handy to refer to the quadrants in terms of these colors. Since the text of this book is in black and white, however, we do not refer to the colors as we explain the framework, but leaders may find them handy as they use the framework in their own organizations.

DYNAMICS

One of the most important applications of the Competing Values Framework is as a guide for change. Hundreds of organizations have used the framework to diagnose and implement culture change, establish competitive strategy, motivate employees, facilitate organizational development and change, implement quality processes, develop high potential leaders, and so on. Using the framework to guide change initiatives has uncovered the existence of two secondary dimensions. These dimensions can help guide the improvement in performance and create value.

One of these secondary dimensions identifies key differences in dynamics, or approaches to change. Specifically, think of a continuum stretching from the upper right quadrant in the framework to the lower left quadrant. This continuum separates an emphasis on change that is new, innovative, unique, and transformational from small incremental change that emphasizes efficiency, predictability, and continuity in the lower left quadrant. This continuum separates a focus on the new from a focus on the better. Some organizations such as Cisco and 3M create value by focusing primarily on new product development and creating new market niches (being new), whereas other organizations such as CH2MHill and Wal-Mart focus primarily on rationalizing processes and continuously improving existing services and delivery systems (being better).

Now think of a continuum stretching from the lower right quadrant to the upper left quadrant. This continuum separates an emphasis on fast, short-term, immediate change (lower right) from an emphasis on long-term, developmental, sustained change (upper left). This continuum separates a focus on speed from a focus on long-term development. Companies celebrated by *Fast Company Magazine* or *Inc. Magazine*, for example, are recognized because of their emphasis on reducing cycle times and producing value in ever more rapid time frames. Speed drives value creation activities. By contrast, firms such as McDonalds, Rubbermaid, Walgreen's, and Berkshire Hathaway are recognized for their emphasis on staying power over time and the value they place on endurance and toughness. Resiliency drives value creation. Figure 1.3 illustrates these dimensions.

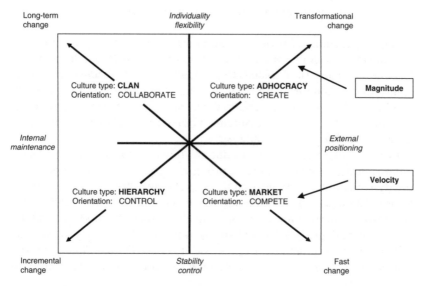

Figure 1.3   Secondary dimensions of the Competing Values Framework –
approaches to change

The dynamics dimension separates value creation strategies on the basis of speed and scope of action. Two key questions addressed are: 'How quickly must we act to create value?' (velocity) And: 'How much change must we initiate to create value?' (magnitude). The velocity of value creation activities separates rapid, short-term value creation (the Compete quadrant) from deliberate, long-term value creation (the Collaborate quadrant), and the magnitude of value creation separates dramatic transformation (creating new value) from incremental improvement (producing increasing value). That is, the Create quadrant is juxtaposed with the Control quadrant by this continuum.

As leaders consider ways in which they must respond to or anticipate opportunities in their organizations, both speed and scope issues represent critical choices upon which value creation will depend. For example, at the beginning of this past decade, Reuters was required to engage in an immediate, rapid-fire transformation in order to reverse the downward spiral of investor confidence that threatened the survival of the firm. High-velocity, large-magnitude change was essential. On the other hand, even in the face of a major threat to its credibility resulting from fictitious stories being passed off as factual news, the *New York Times* approached change efforts in methodical, incremental ways so that a continued foundation of stability and security was maintained. A more deliberate, developmental strategy was pursued.

Rapid-fire, short-term value creation activities (high velocity) focus on immediate, measurable results typical of the Compete quadrant. Long-term development (low velocity), on the other hand, focuses on sustainability and qualitative improvement, more typical of the Collaborate quadrant. Measurement criteria in the former case are often objective and quantitative, whereas the measurement criteria in the latter case are more likely to be subjective or qualitative.

Incremental contributions to value creation (low magnitude) emphasize improving and enhancing existing processes, products, and services as continuity is maintained, typical of the Control quadrant. Breakthrough or transformational value creation (high magnitude), on the other hand, emphasizes radical innovations and extending processes, products, and services into previously unexplored arenas, which typify the Create quadrant. Measurement criteria in the former case are easier to quantify and record, whereas measurement criteria in the latter case often need to be invented or created anew.

LEVEL OF ANALYSIS

A second supplemental dimension in the Competing Values Framework refers to the different levels of analysis that it is also useful for leaders who desire to create value to consider. Whereas the issue of level of analysis is not unique to the Competing Values Framework and has been of central concern in management and organizational studies for decades (Cameron, 1980), the Competing Values Framework highlights the need for congruence among individual dynamics, organizational dynamics, and different types of outcomes associated with value creation. Figure 1.4 illustrates the dimension relating to levels of analysis.

The figure highlights three major levels of analysis – an external outcomes level, an internal organization level, and an individual level. Each level emphasizes different elements in value creation which, when aligned in a congruent way, reinforce and enhance one another.

For example, in Figure 1.4, the outside layer illustrates factors that relate to valued external outcomes produced by the organization, such as customer loyalty, innovative products, shareholder return, brand identity, or global competitiveness. These outcomes refer to different kinds of value created by organizations that have an effect beyond the boundaries of the organization itself. They stand in contrast to the internally-focused outcomes that are often used to determine effectiveness – sales, profits, or efficiency.

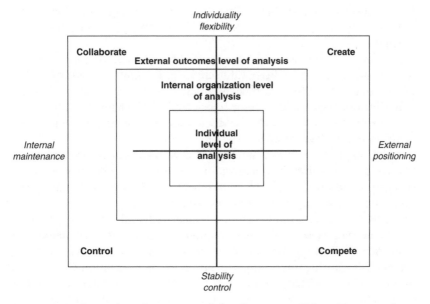

*Figure 1.4   Secondary dimensions of the Competing Values Framework –
levels of analysis*

The Competing Values Framework makes clear that achieving valued
outcomes in each of the quadrants is crucial for organizational effectiveness
over the long term. Leaders should consider multiple outcomes in each of
the quadrants, in other words, as they pursue value creation strategies.
Narrowly defining value to include only financial outcomes, for example,
often ends up producing only short-term results while compromising long-
term value creation. Research findings that confirm this conclusion are
explained in Chapter 6. The development of a well-rounded outcomes portfolio (Gadiesh and Gilbert, 1998) guided by the Competing Values
Framework, in other words, is an important prescription for ensuring long-
term success and value enhancement. More is also said about this prescription in Chapter 6.

This does not mean that all organizations must be equally balanced in all
four quadrants to be successful. An organization such as Dell focused traditionally on mastery in the Control and Compete quadrants to create value.
As conditions changed, however, competencies in other quadrants became
important for sustaining value creation. For example, Dell had to creatively
adapt to declining PC sales and sagging employee morale in 2003. It did so
by becoming more innovative in marketing and outsourcing processes (the
Create quadrant), and by reformulating the office of the CEO (appointing

Kevin Rawlins as CEO) and the organization's global culture. It created a more collaborative culture to balance the company's Control/Compete strengths.

The 'internal organizational level of analysis' refers to elements inside the organization that facilitate value creation. Examples include organizational design, the cultural profile, production processes, incentive systems, strategic initiatives, and core competencies, all of which must be considered as value creation is pursued. The discussion in Chapter 8 provides more detail about this level of analysis.

The Competing Values Framework helps guide leaders in identifying which elements within the organization – for example, efficiency measures (Control quadrant), employee engagement activities (Collaborate quadrant), innovation strategies (Create quadrant), or approaches to customer service (Compete quadrant) – can be emphasized, and to what degree they should be emphasized as value creation strategies are formulated and implemented. Without such a framework to guide strategies and initiatives, leaders risk ignoring important elements in the value creation process. It is also important to keep in mind that not only must internal dynamics in each quadrant be considered, but the congruence between organizational factors and desired outcomes must also be aligned.

The 'individual level of analysis' refers to factors such as personal leadership competencies, learning styles, skills and abilities, and attitudes that are associated with the individuals in the organization. These factors focus on the attributes of individual members in the organization, as separate from the organization's attributes or outcomes. Developing individual leaders, retaining highly valued employees, and fostering a highly energized workforce require attention to individual attributes, and the Competing Values Framework helps identify the importance of a comprehensive view of individual factors for value creation. Focusing on a single motivational technique, one incentive system, or a lone leadership approach without consideration for other approaches suggested by the remaining quadrants inhibits long-term success. Chapter 7 provides more detail about the development of individual leadership strength in the pursuit of value creation.

In sum, aligning different levels of analysis – as represented by desired external outcomes, internal organizational dynamics, and individual attributes – is an important condition for effective performance and value creation, and using the Competing Values Framework to help organize those elements makes the alignment more straightforward and unambiguous. The different levels of analysis should each be considered in value creation activities, and alignment among them is an important part of successful strategy. Considering which level of analysis upon which to focus value creation attempts, in addition to aligning individual competencies with

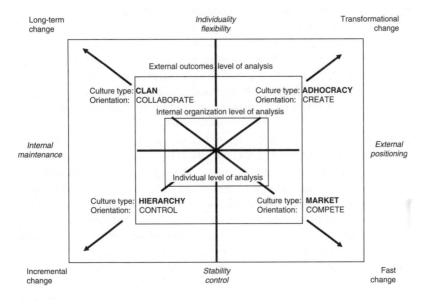

*Figure 1.5   Core and secondary dimensions of the Competing Values
Framework*

organizational capabilities and desired outcomes, are key choices of leaders
wishing to increase value.

Figure 1.5 summarizes the core and secondary dimensions of the
Competing Values Framework. These dimensions illustrate the trade-offs
and tensions inherent in value creation activities, and they highlight the
comprehensive nature of effective leadership when value creation and
effective performance are the desired results.

AN ILLUSTRATION OF COMPETING VALUES

In 1937, Kiichiro Toyoda founded the Toyota Motor Company in Japan as
a spin-off from Toyoda Automatic Loom Works to manufacture cars
roughly based on the designs of Chrysler and Chevrolet. Toyota emerged
from the rubble of war in the late 1950s to become Asia's premiere manufacturing company and swiftly moved from a regional to a global brand.
Gaining a foothold in the United States during the oil embargo of the
1970s, Toyota systematically extended its product array from compact cars,
like the Corolla, to mid-size sedans. In the late 1980s, Toyota accomplished
the previously unimaginable by successfully introducing Lexus, a luxury car

line to compete with European bluebloods, BMW and Mercedes. In fact, the newly introduced Lexus established previously unimaginable initial quality records, and may be said to have been the car that most sparked the quality revolution in the North American auto industry. At the time, the initial quality level for luxury automobiles averaged approximately 148 defects per 100 cars. The first Lexus introduced had an initial quality record of 79 defects per 100 cars . . . an almost unbelievable achievement. Today, Toyota is Japan's biggest carmaker with over $120 billion in annual sales.

Toyota is one the few companies that has demonstrated an ability to pursue several directions simultaneously. The traditional organizational identity at Toyota was highly control focused and internally directed. Perfecting 'lean production' and 'just in time' manufacturing techniques, Toyota became symbolized by quality and efficiency which made it a benchmark for automobile manufacturing worldwide. Engineering, extensive product testing, and process redesign are competencies for which Toyota has become renowned. More recently, Toyota became more adaptive in order to respond to external challenges confronting the firm. In the face of internal calls for protectionism, Toyota diversified its manufacturing and assembly plants from its core location in Toyota City in Aichi, Japan, to new plants in many regions of the world. To survive the worldwide recession and Asian currency crisis of the late 1990s, Toyota introduced innovative 'flexible platform' manufacturing to manage global supply and demand for their products at optimal prices regardless of currency fluctuations. Recently, Toyota has also ventured into non-auto areas such as financial services, and it now runs the Internet portal, Gazoo.com.

The value creation story of Toyota represents both ends of the core dimensions and dynamics of the Competing Values Framework. Toyota's initial approach to value creation was characterized by internally focused, incremental, and control oriented activities. Fine-tuning production and reducing defects were chief areas of concern. Thereafter, however, the introduction of a luxury car – which exceeded by a substantial margin the quality and design standards of competitors in Europe and the United States – coupled with a dramatically successful global manufacturing and distribution strategy and a rapid automobile design process, put Toyota squarely on the opposite side of the dimensions and dynamics continua. The company, in other words, created value by responding simultaneously to competing tensions and opposites. It was both fast and slow, incremental and transformational. It created value with flexibility and anticipation as well as with stability and control. It exemplifies a focus on both internal and external concerns. It focused on the future and the past, the short-run and the long-run, quick results and long-lasting results, change and stability, transformation and incrementalism.

Summary

This brief overview of the core and secondary dimensions that comprise the Competing Values Framework introduces a way to think about creating value in organizations. It helps uncover the simple structure of value creation. It helps explain why companies such as Toyota have enjoyed such dramatic success. The remainder of the book helps clarify how, by utilizing the Competing Values Framework, leaders can enhance their own and their organization's effectiveness and increase value. Considering paradoxical tensions simultaneously, aligning multiple levels of analysis, and thinking in expanded ways about synchronizing opposites are examples of ways in which leaders can improve their effectiveness by utilizing this framework, and a more exhaustive discussion will follow in the remaining chapters.

A ROADMAP FOR THE BOOK

In the remaining chapters, we explain the Competing Values Framework in more detail, including an elaboration of how positively deviant results, or extraordinary levels of success, can be produced. We identify three different approaches to leadership related to the Competing Values Framework: either/or strategies, both/and strategies, and interpenetration strategies. We also provide instruments and measurement devices that can help managers and leaders diagnose and measure the value creation processes, competencies, and outcomes in their own organizations. The book contains intervention tools and techniques designed to enhance and improve value creation in organizations, as well as a discussion of financial measurement devices for assessing value creation. These tools, techniques, and approaches are designed to help leaders develop ways to think about the challenges of leadership, effectiveness, and value creation.

More specifically, in Chapter 2 we discuss the meaning of value, and we identify the challenges inherent in value creation as well as the need to think beyond mere financial value as an indicator of organizational effectiveness. Chapter 3 explains the primary characteristics of the four Competing Values Framework quadrants in order to demonstrate the necessity of considering trade-offs and tensions in creating value. Chapter 4 shifts from a focus on either/or thinking and competing demands to a both/and way of thinking about value creation. Chapter 5 supplements the discussions in the previous two chapters by identifying how the Competing Values Framework can help leaders create new ways to think, new strategies to lead, and new ways to create value.

The second half of the book focuses on tools and techniques for applying the Competing Values Framework. Chapter 6 discusses the tools and techniques that can predict financial performance and the increase of shareholder value. Research comparing organizations' financial performance using the Competing Values Framework to organizations that do not, is reported. Chapter 7 contains measurement devices to assess individual leadership competencies, organizational culture, change strategies, and performance outcomes using the Competing Values Framework. These measurement tools can be useful to leaders in organizations responsible for designing strategies, implementing change processes, and managing cultural transformations. Chapter 8 provides leadership tools and techniques designed to help organizations excel in value creation. Examples of extraordinarily successful performance are provided resulting from the application of these tools and techniques in organizations. Chapter 9 provides a summary of the Competing Values Framework and identifies implications for leaders of the future.

2. Clarifying the meaning of value

Before we continue with our discussion of the underlying structure and implications of the Competing Values Framework, we want to briefly discuss what we mean by value creation. Because creating value is the ultimate objective of leadership and effective organizational performance (illustrated by Figure 1.1), clarifying the meaning of value and explaining how the framework is used by leaders to enhance value creation is necessary. In other words, we must address the question, 'What is value, and why must leaders care about value creation for their organizations?'

The chief reason that people are employed by the organizations in which they work is because the benefits they produce for their organizations exceed the cost to the organizations of producing those benefits. Viewed from this perspective, people are value creators in organizations when the value of what they generate exceeds the value of what they consume. They create value when they increase the flow of benefits being produced for organizations, or when they reduce the amount of resources being consumed to produce those benefits. Producing more benefit than cost makes them value creators. This value may take the form of products or services, meaningfulness in work, expanded opportunities, personal energy, positive example, interpersonal support, and so forth.

Similarly, organizations create value when the products and services being produced provide greater benefits to customers than the costs of producing those products and services. When organizations achieve the goals expected by shareholders, sponsors, customers, and other stakeholders, and the costs to those groups is less than the benefits received, value has been created by the organization.

Individuals who get ahead the fastest, have the greatest energy and enthusiasm, and are the happiest at work are typically those who are the most effective value creators (Thakor, 2000). Moreover, the organizations that consistently outperform others are also those with the most value-creating individuals (Dutton, 2003). In effect, creating value is a primary motivation that drives both individuals and organizations. At a personal level, having a positive impact and making a contribution in an area of personal significance is one of the most basic of human needs. Creating value is the way people achieve self-fulfillment and realize their unique potential (Lawrence and Nohria, 2002).

Similarly, all organizations exist to create value, whether they are corporations, churches, schools, or government agencies. Employees, families, customers, stakeholders, and the broader community all receive value from organizations; otherwise there is little reason for them to survive. Of course, what represents value for one organization may not represent value for another. For a publicly traded company, for example, value is linked to financial returns that the company delivers to its shareholders. For a nonprofit educational institution, value is linked to the quality of students' educational experience and their preparation for the future. For a hospital, value is tied to the quality of health care that leads to patient recovery. In each case, the extent to which value is created is the chief predictor of organizational success. The more value created, the more valuable the organization, and the more the organization is likely to succeed over the long run.

THE PROBLEM WITH VALUE

A chief concern of researchers and leaders has been to identify a framework that can explain how organizations create value. In parallel, they have tried to develop assessment tools to accurately measure the creation of value. This has been no small task as people disagree on what aspect of value creation is the most important to assess. Some emphasize human concerns, whereas others emphasize environmental sustainability. Some advocate financial capital, whereas others advocate intellectual capital. The ultimate aim of those trying to explain value creation has been to discover a way to predict *future* value creation. Knowing in advance which organizations will do well and which will not is akin to predicting the winner of the Super Bowl. Everyone would like to know in advance who will do well and who will not.

The problem is, identifying, measuring, and predicting value is very challenging. First, rapid, dynamic, and dramatic change in the modern environment makes value creation an inherently ambiguous process. Trying to understand and measure a moving target is difficult, at best. The rules of value creation have changed markedly in the last several years, and processes and technologies that have not created value in the past are emerging as the key drivers of value in the future. For example, efficiency and productivity were keys to financial success in the decades after World War II, whereas innovation and entrepreneurship have become more central value drivers in the twenty-first century. Second, the traditional measures of value creation, as captured on corporate balance sheets, work less well in today's economy. Instead of being adequately indicated by traditional financial ratios, value creation is often represented by hard-to-measure soft factors such as knowledge assets, innovation, and human capital. Third, tools for creating, measuring, and predicting value have typically been developed in isolation from one another, despite their interconnections. For example, value creation approaches like strategy formulation, organization redesign, leadership development, human resource training, culture change initiatives, and improved resource allocation processes have not been encapsulated in a congruent whole. Approaches to measuring value typically have involved financial metrics like Economic Value Added (EVA) and Return on Assets or Return on Investment (ROA, ROI), but no systematic integration has emerged among these various measures. Predicting value creation has included a host of statistical forecasting tools such as time-series analysis, stock price charting and so on, but these do not explain the underlying determinants of value creation.

The problem with developing a dynamic, comprehensive, integrated model for value creation is illustrated by a metaphor. Specifically, discovering the best approach to value creation is in many ways similar to the voyage of Christopher Columbus in search of the best route to Asia.

Columbus was an entrepreneur as well as a sailor from Genoa who sought financing for a highly speculative expedition to find a shorter western route to the spice trade in India. For years he had solicited funds from several of the monarchs around the Mediterranean who deemed his idea too risky and uncertain. They took this position with good reason. Several other European expeditions had attempted this feat with disastrous results.

As a sailor, Columbus knew that the world was round, as did many navigators in the fifteenth century. What they didn't know was the distance between Europe and Asia, since no one was certain of the circumference of the globe. In fact, India, China, and Indonesia (the Spice Islands) were considered by many leading cartographers to be in the same, immediate vicinity. Columbus knew nothing about the food available, wind and weather conditions, or the relative hospitality of the native inhabitants. So, like anyone who goes on a journey of discovery to undiscovered territory, he hedged his bets by diversifying his approach.

In high-risk situations, it is customary to reduce the resources allocated to the challenge in order to reduce the risk of loss. Value is created by minimizing the costs of failure. Yet, Columbus did the opposite. He convinced King Ferdinand and Queen Isabella of Spain to give him three ships instead of one: *Niña*, *Pinta*, and *Santa Maria*. Each ship was a different size with its own unique rigging, provisions, and crew. Creating value when the pathway is certain usually involves optimizing efficiency to get to the destination cheaper and faster. The emphasis is usually on reducing variance and on maintaining control. When the path is uncertain, however, diversifying and learning through trial and error is usually more effective. That is, conducting a series of mini-experiments to see what works as the pathway unfolds is a less efficient but more enlightening approach. That is exactly what Columbus did as he navigated his three ships in a serpentine pattern westward.

When Columbus accidentally landed in the Caribbean, he and his crew discovered it was not full of spices or anything of apparent value. Moreover, one of the ships broke rank and sailed off to look for gold, while the flagship ran aground on a reef and sank. Bad winds and ill fate took Columbus back to Spain on his only remaining ship. For their investment, the King and Queen of Spain received no spices or gold, but only the smallest weather-beaten vessel in return.

The story of Columbus illustrates a contemporary dilemma of value creation: was the voyage of Columbus a success or a failure? Would the modern day stock market reward such an enterprise? If one evaluates the value of the voyage in terms of its immediate investment (ROI), it was a categorical failure. A large number of assets were poured into the project with little financial return. On the other hand, if the value of the voyage is evaluated from the perspective of developing competency to create other desired outcomes, it was a resounding success. In fact, the project was such a success that, after Columbus's voyage, the Spanish established the most viable trade routes to the New World and colonized it to the great advantage of the empire. Large convoys from Spain made their way westward with less risk and more return using the maps Columbus had created during his initial voyage.

In other words, the value created by the Columbus adventure was different from the traditional measures of financial return. The greatest value created by this exploratory journey was a universal standard by which the world could be easily mapped. Techniques such as dead-reckoning – where a rope with knots is tossed overboard while someone counts off the number of seconds it takes for the length to be unfurled – and celestial navigation – where sextant and compass are used to sail toward stars – were the essential navigational tools available to Columbus. Time, speed, and distance were calculated as the vessel moved along. However, in the ensuing centuries, thanks in no small measure to Columbus' efforts, uniform standards for latitude and longitude were developed and global navigation and world trade became a reality. In essence, Columbus' map – a way of recognizing new destinations and routes – was more valuable than any treasure he brought back from his voyages. He created the *capability* to discover new opportunities.

Similarly, organizations that rely of traditional indicators of value – or that adopt non-integrated approaches to creating, measuring, and predicting value creation – inadvertently foster within their organizations the pursuit of disparate, disjointed, or even contradictory initiatives. Predictably, they usually fail to achieve their desired objectives.

In contrast, the Competing Values Framework advocates an integrated and comprehensive approach to value creation which uncovers many alternatives to traditional financial measures of value. Financial return is crucial, of course, but a single-minded focus on monetary value almost always spells disaster for organizations and individuals alike. Like Columbus, heterogeneity in indicators and creators of value almost always lead to more successful outcomes.

EXAMPLES OF APPLYING THE COMPETING VALUES FRAMEWORK

As mentioned in Chapter 1, the Competing Values Framework has been used in a variety of organizational types and for a variety of purposes. Change projects, assessment tasks, leadership development opportunities, and turnaround assignments have all relied on the Competing Values Framework as an approach for achieving organizational effectiveness and value creation. Three such cases are briefly described here as an illustration of the practical utility of the framework. In each instance, these organizations were seeking improvement of financial value, but a variety of types of additional value was also necessary for them to succeed. Each case briefly illustrates the use of the Competing Values Framework as an intervention approach for creating multiple types of value.

Philips Electronics

For the first time in its history, Philips Electronics lost money in 1992. This is one of Europe's, and the world's, most venerated firms with operations in more than 150 countries and employing more than a quarter of a million employees. Philips has produced 10 000 inventions and holds more than 60 000 patents (including well-known products such as audiocassettes, laser discs, and compact discs). The company held the number 1, 2, or 3 position in worldwide market share in lighting, consumer electronics, computer and television monitors, CDs for music, shavers, coffeemakers, color television tubes, medical imaging equipment, X-ray equipment, and digitization equipment. It was a firm that had simply never experienced red ink in more than a century of existence.

The early 1990s, however, brought a very real threat of bankruptcy and, predictably, a significant change in the firm's leadership, strategy, and measurement systems. A new CEO was hired – Jan Timmer – and a set of change initiatives were instituted that led to a dramatic turnaround in profitability and stock price. Improvements of more than 120 percent in firm valuation were realized over the next five years. This remarkable recovery resulted to a substantial degree from the conscious application of a Competing Values Framework. Labeled 'Centurion,' the turnaround program included putting into place strategic actions, leadership development programs, and measurement systems that were guided by this framework. Leaders relied on the framework to determine appropriate measures of success, key managerial and leadership competencies, financial investment strategies, and competitive global initiatives. Key value creation initiatives in each of the quadrants were highlighted, and, for the first time, a congruent and consistent approach to value creation was used through multiple levels of the company.

Dana Corporation

Up until the late-1980s, Dana Corporation – one of the world's largest automotive suppliers with operations in 32 countries worldwide – did not have a systematic quality program operating in the company. To be fair, its focus as a firm was on achieving 'excellence,' and its products and services were considered to be among the best in the industry. Moreover, for the most part, automotive manufacturers were satisfied with Dana's performance. The Japanese invasion of the U.S. automotive industry in the 1980s, however, revealed levels of quality and productivity that markedly exceeded those of most U.S. manufacturing companies, including Dana. The need for a revolution in quality processes was clearly evident. If Dana was to maintain its place as one of the world's leaders in the industry, it had to pay attention to quality in a systematic and rigorous way.

The approach to quality implemented by Dana beginning in 1992 was not merely a piecemeal implementation of quality tools and techniques – for example, quality circles, fishbone diagrams, kaizen principles, six-sigma techniques (which are initiatives to improve quality, cut costs and increase consistency pioneered by leading Japanese companies in the 1970s and 1980s). Rather, it was driven by a zealous commitment on the part of the CEO – Woody Morcott – to the Competing Values Framework. Quality was approached as a comprehensive, integrated strategy that touched almost every facet of the company. Quality process, practices, and indicators in each of the four quadrants differentiated Dana's quality approach from others in the auto supply industry. This application of the Competing Values Framework – including leadership development, measurement, strategy, creativity, and standards – resulted in Dana winning a Malcolm Baldrige National Quality Award in 1995 and again in 2000 as well as recognition as one of *Industry Week*'s 100 best managed companies in 1998 and 1999.

Reuters

Reuters is a 157-year-old British firm with a reputation for honest, fair, and accurate news reporting. The name Reuters is associated with reliability and trustworthiness throughout the world in print and television media. The trouble is, only about 10 percent of the annual revenues for Reuters come from the news business. Approximately 90 percent of the business is associated with Reuters' financial information service – selling terminals, providing networking for financial markets, and delivering up-to-date and accurate market information used by financial analysts throughout the world. By the late 1990s, Bloomburg's entry into the financial markets business had created major erosion in Reuters' top-end business, and Thompson's low-end, bare-bones entry strategy created pressure on Reuters inexpensive, basic services. The company found itself being squeezed in the middle with profitability taking a beating. The survival of the firm, in fact, was in real question when Tom Glocer took the reigns as CEO in 2002.

Glocer was instrumental in adopting an approach to turnaround that relied centrally on the Competing Values Framework. Multiple initiatives including cost containment strategies (Control quadrant), new product development programs (Create quadrant), competitive initiatives and strategic alliances with firms such as AOL (Compete quadrant), and strong leadership and human capacity development activities (Collaborate quadrant) were instituted almost immediately. This comprehensive initiative was labeled by the acronym, *FAST*, but it not only focused on immediate results but on putting a foundation in place that would create value over the long-term. The Competing Values Framework helped guide the turnaround strategies (i.e., immediate, long-term, better, and new strategies) which resulted not only in the survival of Reuters but in enhanced value creation that signaled a dramatic turnaround success.

Rocky Flats

Sixteen miles west of Denver a nuclear weapons production facility had been in operation since 1951, producing a majority of the nuclear triggers during the Cold War. An engineering and environmental firm, CH2MHill received a contract in 1995 to close down the facility and clean up all of the radioactive pollution that had occurred on the 6000-acre site over the previous half century. The Department of Energy estimated that the clean up would take at least 70 years, and the budget allocated for the task was $36 billion. Upon arrival in 1995, CH2MHill found an antagonistic union-ized workforce as indicated by 900 grievances, a secret and secure facility surrounded by two razor wire fences, prison-like watch towers, and submachine-gun-armed security guards to prevent suicide mission entrants or other subversives. The site was more polluted than any other nuclear facility in America, with more than 21 tons of weapons-grade nuclear material present, at least 100 tons of high content plutonium residues with no treatment or disposal path, 30 000 liters of plutonium and enriched uranium solutions stored in leaky tanks and pipes, more than 258 000 cubic meters of low-level radioactive waste and nearly 15 000 cubic meters of transuranic waste stored in 39 500 containers. A special *Nightline* television program rated two Rocky Flats buildings as 'the most dangerous buildings in America' due to their levels of radioactive pollution. Long-running battles had been fought historically between Rocky Flats and government regulatory agencies, environmental groups, community representatives, and concerned citizens. The facility was almost in a state of siege by outside agencies and a concerned citizenry.

In light of these ominous challenges, the prospects of a successful closure and clean-up of Rocky Flats in the 70-year time frame were dim. Yet, through a systematic application of the Competing Values Framework (see Cameron and Lavine, 2006) the entire project was completed 60 years early and at a $30 billion saving in taxpayer funds. All 800 buildings were demol-ished, all radioactive waste removed, and soil and water remediated to better-than-federal standards in a fraction of the estimated time. The cost for the project was $3.9 billion ($7.1 billion in total, including the years before CH2MHill took over the project), a small fraction of the federally budgeted amount. Most antagonists such as citizen action groups, envi-ronmentalists, community mayors, and state regulators transitioned from protestors and adversaries to being advocates, lobbyists, and partners. Labor relations among the three unions (i.e., steelworkers, security guards, building trades) improved from 900 grievances to a mere handful per year, and a culture of life-long employment and employee entitlement was replaced by a workforce that enthusiastically worked itself out of a job as quickly as possible. Remediated pollution levels surpassed federal stan-dards by a multiple of 13, and safety performance exceeded federal stan-dards twofold and the construction industry average fourfold. More than 200 technological innovations were produced in the service of faster and safer performance.

These four brief examples illustrate dramatic improvement in the creation of multiple kinds of value as a result of the application of the Competing Values Framework. Of course, our brief overview of this framework up to this point is not comprehensive enough to explain these results. Instead, it is meant merely to introduce some of the rudiments of the Competing Values Framework and to illustrate its potential for leaders who want to improve effectiveness and create value. The remaining chapters explain in more detail how the framework can be used by leaders, and they report empirical results that confirm its power in addressing real organizational challenges.

WHAT THEN DO WE MEAN BY VALUE?

The earlier discussion in this chapter suggested that value can be created by an organization in one of four ways, and that value is created whenever an organization develops competencies in Control, Compete, Create and Collaborate that collectively generate output that exceeds what individuals (or subunits within the organization) could do on their own. In other words, value is created when every stakeholder is made better off (or at least as well off) than he or she would be without the organization. That is, employees are better off than they would be on their own (Collaborate competency), internal processes help coordinate activities better than individuals could achieve on their own (Control competency), and customers and shareholders are better off than they would be without the firm (Compete and Create competencies). This notion of value creation is consistent with how the stock market values firms. Value is created whenever the firm delivers shareholder returns that exceed the risk-adjusted expected returns shareholders can get on their own (their opportunity cost of capital). The additional insight of the Competing Values Framework is in explaining the ways in which such value is created for shareholders and other stakeholders.

3. The quadrants in the Competing Values Framework

It is not news that we live in a dynamic, turbulent, chaotic world. Almost no one would try to predict with any degree of certainty what the world will be like in ten years. Things change too fast. We know that the technology currently exists, for example, to put the equivalent of a full-size computer in a wristwatch, or inject the equivalent of a laptop computer into the bloodstream. New computers will probably be etched on molecules instead of silicone wafers. The mapping of the human genome is probably the greatest source for change, for not only can we now change a banana into an agent to inoculate people against malaria, but new organ development and physiological regulation promises to dramatically alter population life styles. Who can predict the changes that will result? Thus, not only is change currently ubiquitous and constant, but almost everyone predicts that it will escalate exponentially.

The trouble is, when everything is changing, it is impossible to manage change. Let's say you're flying an airplane, for example, moving through the air. Everything is changing. You're constantly moving. The trouble is, it is impossible to guide the plane unless you can find a fixed point, something that doesn't change. You cannot control the plane if everything is in motion. Consider the last flight of John Kennedy, Jr., for example, who began to fly at dusk up the New England coast. He lost sight of land and, because it got dark, of the horizon line as well. He lost his fixed point. The result was disorientation, and he flew his plane into the ocean, probably without knowing he was headed towards water. He couldn't manage change without a stable reference – an immutable, universal, unchanging standard (see Cameron, 2006).

When things are unstable – i.e., an absence of fixed points, dependable principles, or stable benchmarks – people tend to make up their own rules. Without a sense-making framework that helps put into alignment the chaos of the ever-changing environment, people often make sense in ineffective ways. Consider, for example, the high pressure, high velocity environments that exist in the energy-trading, telecommunications, and accounting industries. In several infamous instances, people cheated, lied, or waffled not only because it was to their economic advantage, but because they had created their own rationale for what was acceptable and what was real. They lost sight of fixed points. One key function of the Competing Values Framework is to make it possible to interpret a turbulent and ambiguous environment in a consistent and effective way. The framework permits people to align disparate and dynamic factors in the environment in ways that create value rather than destroy value.

In this sense, the Competing Values Framework is an approach to thinking – that is, to interpreting or making sense of complex phenomena – as well as to developing a repertoire of competencies and strategies that address the complexities being encountered. In this chapter we discuss in more detail the quadrants of the Competing Values Framework that are formed by the two primary dimensions. We identify their key attributes and important implications. Our purpose is to help leaders develop a way to think about complex and ambiguous issues by making a systematic framework accessible and usable. The framework can serve as the fixed point, the stable interpretation system, which allows for effective leadership in conditions of dynamic change.

QUADRANTS

In Chapter 1 we explained that the Competing Values Framework is based on sets of primary and secondary dimensions derived from scholarly research and managerial practice. These dimensions differentiate emphases that oppose one another or that represent contradictory approaches to value creation. The core vertical and horizontal dimensions produce four quadrants, each of which organizes and categorizes a collection of strategies, competencies, and perspectives that leaders may use to foster value creation. Understanding these quadrants is probably the most important aspect of the entire Competing Values Framework, so we will discuss them in some detail here.

Each quadrant is labeled with an action verb connoting the kinds of value creating activities that characterize it – Collaborate, Create, Compete, and Control. Leaders and organizations that create the greatest amount of value have developed high degrees of competency in one or more of these four quadrants. That is, each quadrant represents a way of thinking about opportunities and challenges, an approach to address them, and a set of strategies and tactics that foster value creation in organizations. Figure 3.1 summarizes some of the key attributes of each quadrant.

A great deal of research has confirmed that leaders and organizations gravitate toward one or more of these quadrants over time (Cameron and Quinn, 2006). For leaders this means that they develop a specific set of

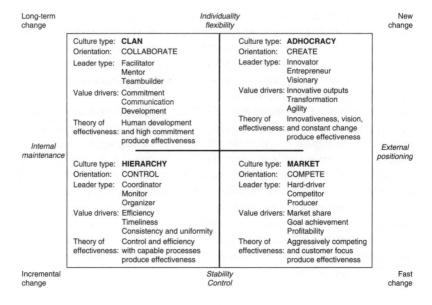

Long-term   Individuality   New
change   flexibility   change

Culture type: **CLAN**	Culture type: **ADHOCRACY**
Orientation: COLLABORATE	Orientation: CREATE
Leader type: Facilitator / Mentor / Teambuilder	Leader type: Innovator / Entrepreneur / Visionary
Value drivers: Commitment / Communication / Development	Value drivers: Innovative outputs / Transformation / Agility
Theory of effectiveness: Human development and high commitment produce effectiveness	Theory of effectiveness: Innovativeness, vision, and constant change produce effectiveness

Internal   External
maintenance   positioning

Culture type: **HIERARCHY**	Culture type: **MARKET**
Orientation: CONTROL	Orientation: COMPETE
Leader type: Coordinator / Monitor / Organizer	Leader type: Hard-driver / Competitor / Producer
Value drivers: Efficiency / Timeliness / Consistency and uniformity	Value drivers: Market share / Goal achievement / Profitability
Theory of effectiveness: Control and efficiency with capable processes produce effectiveness	Theory of effectiveness: Aggressively competing and customer focus produce effectiveness

Incremental   Stability   Fast
change   Control   change

Figure 3.1   The Competing Values Framework – culture, leadership, value drivers, and effectiveness

skills and areas of expertise. They develop mental models as well as behavioral competencies that become biased toward one or more of these quadrants. For organizations it means that they develop a dominant culture, a set of core competencies, and a strategic intent that are characterized by one or more of the quadrants. The Competing Values Framework helps leaders and organizations diagnose and interpret these styles and inclinations and to utilize them in value creation activities. Developing an understanding of, and competency in, the attributes and activities represented in each quadrant is an important key to effective performance. The information included here comes from both empirical research studies as well as numerous organizational interventions using the competing values approach. Let's begin with the lower left quadrant of Figure 3.1.

The Control Quadrant

Value-enhancing activities in the Control quadrant include pursuing improvements in efficiency by implementing better processes. A mantra for this quadrant might be: 'better, cheaper, and surer.' Possessing a substantial degree of statistical predictability is one of the hallmarks of this quadrant. Organizational effectiveness is associated with capable processes, measurement, and control. Examples of activities relating to value creation in the Control quadrant include quality enhancements such as statistical process control and other quality control processes like six-sigma, cost and productivity improvements, reduction in manufacturing cycle time, and efficiency enhancement measures. These activities help make organizations function more smoothly and efficiently.

Leadership strategies in this quadrant help eliminate errors and increase the regularity and consistency of outcomes. The quadrant includes inwardly focused, disciplined strategies concerned with improving efficiency and cutting costs out of production. The extensive use of processes, systems, and technology are hallmarks of this quadrant. The use of standardized procedures and an emphasis on rule-reinforcement and uniformity predominate.

Activities anchored in the Control quadrant create the most value when failure is not an option – as in industries such as medicine, nuclear power, military services, and transportation – or in highly regulated or stable environments. Value results primarily from increasing certainty, predictability, and regularity, and by eliminating anything that inhibits a perfect or error-free outcome. Adopting enhanced measurement systems, downsizing, and divesting unproductive units all are Control quadrant activities.

Leaders who are most competent in the Control quadrant tend to be organizers and administrators. They pay attention to details, make careful decisions, are precise in their analyses, and focus on one best way. They tend to be conservative, cautious, and logical as problem solvers where procedures are followed methodically, and persistence highlights their style. They are often technical experts and well informed. They keep track of details and obtain power based on information control and technical expertise. Documentation and information management are actively pursued.

Value creation through control competencies – Dell

There are few companies that have created as much value through a single-minded focus on a new business design as Dell has. The business design, predicated on direct PC sales to consumers rather than through the traditional distribution channels, is stunning in its simplicity and has allowed Dell to not only generate enormous value for its shareholders and customers, but also transform the computer industry. At the end of 2003, Dell was trading at a price–earnings multiple of 40, which was much higher than the overall stock market and other stellar firms like Microsoft, GE and Wal-Mart.

There are three keys to Dell's success. First, its direct-sell model contains a business process improvement that permits Dell to not only sell PCs cheaper to customers but also achieve extremely low levels of working capital and high levels of asset turnover. Second, Dell focuses relentlessly on cost efficiencies and operating margin, so that profitability is not sacrificed as higher sales volumes are pursued. Continuous improvement on these dimensions is the norm. And third, the company believes in accountability and employees questioning everything and challenging their bosses. For example, when executives complained about CEO Michael Dell's detached style in 360-degree reviews, he followed-up with personal and organizational changes, that fostered higher levels of engagement.

As is evident, the tools Dell uses to create value come primarily from the Control quadrant. What is interesting, however, is that Dell is also very strong in the Compete quadrant and is beginning to develop strength in the diagonally-opposite Collaborate quadrant.

The Compete Quadrant

Value-enhancing activities in the Compete quadrant include being aggressive and forceful in the pursuit of competitiveness. Organizations that excel in this quadrant emphasize and engender their competitive position. They monitor and scan the signals from the marketplace and on how to deliver shareholder value consistently. Speed is an essential element in maintaining a competitive edge, so results-right-now is a typical demand. A mantra of the Compete quadrant might be: 'compete hard, move fast, and play to win.' Organizational effectiveness is associated with aggressive competition, fast response, and customer focus.

Examples of value creating activities belonging to the Compete quadrant include implementing aggressive measures to expand working capital, outsourcing selected aspects of production or services, acquiring other firms, investing in customer acquisition and customer service activities, and attacking competitor organization's market position. The strategies in this quadrant help position the firm to have a strong standing with investors by creating a superior reputation for delivering excellent financial performance in the immediate term.

Leadership strategies are aimed at producing short-term profitability for shareholders. Customers and clients are of highest priority, and they are defined as the ultimate objective of being in business. Success is judged on the basis of indicators such as market share, revenues, meeting budget targets, and growth in profitability. Rapid response and speed of action are hallmarks of value creating activities, and the philosophies of former Chrysler Chairman Lee Iacocca, 'Lead, follow, or get out of the way,' and former General Electric Chairman Jack Welch, 'Control your destiny or someone else will,' are typical of the Compete quadrant leadership approach. Taking charge, moving fast, and being aggressive are typical values.

Strategies in the Compete quadrant create the most value when organizations must manage a portfolio of initiatives, financial partnerships, acquisitions, or federation agreements. Intense levels of pressure to perform – for example, by financial analysts or shareholders – motivate organizations to emphasize the Compete quadrant. Delivering results, making fast decisions, driving through barriers to achieve results, and building a profit focus all typify the orientation that leaders adopt in their pursuit of value creation.

Individual leaders tend to be hard driving, directive, and competitive. They welcome challenges and stretch goals and have high levels of achievement orientation. Type A personalities (Friedman, 1996), assertive behavior, and strong wills characterize Compete quadrant managers. Their power and success are judged on the basis of results, not through their level of effort or the methods used.

Value creation through compete competencies – General Dynamics
When former astronaut Bill Anders took over as CEO of General Dynamics in 1991, the defense industry was shrinking dramatically as a consequence of the end of the Cold War. The typical response of companies in such a circumstance is to avoid shrinkage by diversifying outside their core businesses. However, such a strategy has rarely proved successful. Bill Anders adopted a different strategy. His strategy was to:

- Consider divesting any business unit with General Dynamic that could not be either number one or number two in its industry and could not have sufficient scale to justify dedicated factories.
- Lay off employees to downsize wherever needed.
- Focus resources on the remaining businesses.
- Re-engineer executive compensation packages to remove linkages of bonuses to accounting measures of performance and provide instead high-powered incentives that linked executive bonuses to improvements in cash flow and increases in shareholder value.
- Put executives through a week-long education program on shareholder value and managing for cash flow.

As a consequence, in the next few years General Dynamics shrank from a company with over $9 billion in sales to just over $3 billion in sales, but the market value of its equity grew over 300 percent during this time. It is evident that the tools of value creation employed by Anders – divestitures, downsizing and market-dominance criteria to decide where to focus resources – came from the Compete quadrant. However, Anders didn't ignore other quadrants entirely, as evidenced by his focus on executive education and the re-engineering of executive compensation, the diagonally-opposite Collaborate quadrant.

The Create Quadrant

Value-enhancing activities in the Create quadrant deal with innovation in the products and services the organization produces. A mantra of this quadrant might be: 'Create, innovate, and envision the future.'

Organizations that excel in this quadrant effectively handle discontinuity, change, and risk. They allow for freedom of thought and action among employees so that rule breaking and stretching beyond barriers are common characteristics of the organization's culture. Organizational effectiveness is associated with entrepreneurship, vision, and constant change.

Examples of value creating activities in this quadrant include innovative product-line extensions, radical new process breakthroughs (e.g., Polaroid's development of instant photography), innovations in distribution and logistics that redefine entire industries (e.g., Dell, Wal-Mart), and developing new technologies (e.g., gene splicing and quantum computing). Focusing on the strategies in this quadrant enables companies to leapfrog their competitors and achieve breakthrough levels of performance. The risk–return ratio is very different, of course, when pursuing inventive entrepreneurial strategies compared to the strategies associated with the Control and Compete quadrants. The potential payoff is high when creating new value, but so is the probability of failure. Moreover, the pace at which results occur and with which success is achieved is also unpredictable.

Leaders' strategies are aimed at producing new products and services, creating new market niches, and producing value by enhancing the processes by which entrepreneurship can be enhanced in the organization. Elaborating the portfolio of products and services through innovation and helping new ventures process to flourish are key challenges of Create quadrant leaders.

Create quadrant strategies produce the most value in hyper-turbulent, fast moving environments that demand cutting edge ideas and innovations.

Organizations that can predict the future and adapt readily to emerging dynamic conditions will flourish while other organizations are awaiting the uncertainty to diminish. Create quadrant organizations excel at being pioneers and definers of industry or sector trends. Thoughtful experimentation, learning from mistakes, and failing fast (for example, trying out a lot of ideas that probably won't work) in order to succeed more quickly (for example, find the ones that do work) are typical of successful Create quadrant organizations.

Individual leaders who excel in this quadrant tend to be gifted visionaries and futurists, inclined toward risk, and unafraid of uncertainty. They are typically adept at creating fantasy, dreams, and vision for the organization. But those dreams and visions are not merely pie-in-the-sky thinking. The ability to stay abreast of changes, remain imaginative, and undertake original actions makes Create quadrant leaders the darlings of fast-paced industries such as information technology, bio-engineering, and communications.

Value creation through create competencies – W.L. Gore

One of the best innovators is a privately-held company based in Newark, Delaware, called W.L. Gore, which operates in a number of product areas, including guitar strings, dental floss, medical devices and fuel cells (*Fortune*, 2003). The company is best known as the manufacturer of Gore-Tex fabric. It innovates continuously on a lot of different fronts and uses its inventions to keep entering new businesses. How does W.L. Gore do it? Here are the tools the company uses:

- *Use potential customers for help:* The company routinely seeks out potential users of products it is developing to elicit ideas. For example, it sought the help of physicians to create thoracic graft, and hunters to test garments made of a new fabric that blocks human odor.
- *Let employees determine what they want to do:* Gore employees do not have titles or bosses in the conventional sense and work on projects they believe are most worthy of their time. As a result, they tend to be very passionate about what they are doing. Moreover, research associates get to spend 10 percent of their work hours as 'dabble time,' developing their own ideas.
- *Use a diversified innovation approach:* At any one time, Gore typically has hundreds of projects in various stages of development. The company uses a decentralized innovation approach most of the time, and the diversified approach enhances the odds of at least some innovations becoming commercially profitable.
- *Know when to let go:* Since not every innovation turns into a sustainable product, Gore also divests products when it deems appropriate. For example, a Gore associate developed gunk-repelling coating for bike cables. The company did not see much potential in that business but thought the product had potential for use on guitar strings. Elixir, a Gore product, is today the leading brand of acoustic guitar strings in the U.S.

Inspecting Gore's approach to innovation, we see that the company uses tools from a variety of quadrants to be successful in developing its Create competencies. Using customers to help in innovation and knowing when to let go are Compete tools, employees' freedom to innovate in a flat organization is a Collaborate tool, and using a diversified innovation approach is a Create tool.

The Collaborate Quadrant

Value-enhancing activities in the Collaborate quadrant deal with building human competencies, developing people, and solidifying an organizational culture. The approach to change in this quadrant is deliberate and methodical because consensual and cooperative processes rule. A mantra of this competence might be: 'human development, human empowerment, human commitment.' The focus is on building cohesion through consensus and satisfaction through involvement. Organizations succeed because they hire, develop, and retain their human resource base. Organizational effectiveness is associated with human development and high levels of participant engagement.

Examples of activities in this competence include clarifying and reinforcing organizational values, norms, and expectations; developing employees and cross-functional work groups; implementing programs to enhance employee retention; and fostering teamwork and decentralized decision making. Examples include Intel's non-bureaucratic office structure in which all employees (including former-CEO Andrew Grove) work in easily accessible cubicles, the empowering of field managers by CEO Jack Greenberg at McDonald's Corporation, and the large investments in employee training and development by General Electric and Motorola. It is the activities in this quadrant that help to sustain and prolong the capabilities of the organization to create value.

Leaders' strategies are aimed at building the human capacity of the organization. Human and social capital take priority over financial capital because they are assumed to produce financial capital. Interpersonal skills and competent human interaction are crucial prerequisites to value creation in this quadrant, so leadership strategies emphasize the development of effective relationships. A sense of community, a commitment to culture, and a willingness to cooperate are key outcomes of Collaborate quadrant strategies.

Collaborate quadrant strategies produce the most value for organizations when stability must be maintained in the face of uncertainty. Forming effective and long-lasting partnerships across organizational boundaries – inside and outside the organization – is often a requirement for long-term success, and competency in the Collaborate quadrant is the pathway to achieve those ends.

Individual leaders who excel in the Collaborate quadrant tend to take on roles of parent figure, mentor, facilitator, and team builder. They value shared objectives, mutual contribution, and a sense of collectivity among their employees. They produce working environments that are free of conflict and tension, and organization members tend to be more loyal to the organization and to the team than in organizations emphasizing the other quadrants. Helping individuals develop needed skills, ensuring a fit between job requirements and skills, and fostering life balance all are key objectives of Collaborate quadrant leaders regarding the individuals for whom they have responsibility.

Value creation through collaborate competencies – SPX

SPX is a leading manufacturer of tools that automobile manufacturers require that their dealers use when they perform repairs on cars still under warranty. The company also makes electronic diagnostic equipment and emissions-testing equipment for car dealers and auto service centers, as well as a variety of components for the auto industry. In 1995, however, the company was struggling financially, with its stock price hitting a low of $10.75 per share. In the spring of 1995, the company decided to adopt Economic Value Added (EVA) for incentive compensation, performance assessment and resource allocation. In conjunction with this, CEO John Blystone took the following steps:

- Sold its Sealed Power division to Dana Corporation.
- Established collaborative stretch goals for Earnings per share and EVA improvement to achieve targets in one-fifth the time Wall Street was expecting. These stretch goals were established through dialogue with SPX managers.
- Reorganized the company's ten operating divisions into three main product groups with highly integrated strategies.
- Organized monthly presentations by division managers to their peers regarding specific actions they were taking to achieve their goals, best practices, and celebratory events.
- Redesigned the compensation system so that employees were rewarded for improvements in EVA.

As is evidence, SPX achieved its value-creation goals by using a combination of Collaborate and Compete tools. Improving its stock price was a Compete goal and the divestiture of Sealed Power was a move from the Compete quadrant. However, what made SPX's EVA implementation successful were primarily Collaborate tools – the collaborative determination of stretch goals, the sharing of best practices, and the reengineering of the compensation system.

Figure 3.2 summarizes the primary emphases of the four quadrants.

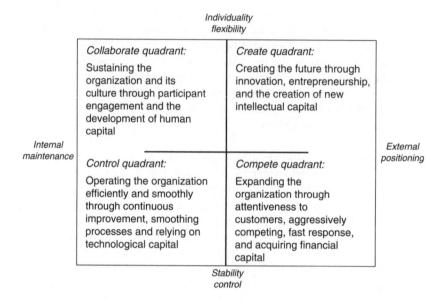

Figure 3.2   Emphases of the four quadrants in the Competing Values Framework

FUNCTIONAL AREAS AND RESOURCE MAPS

Activities in each of the quadrants create value, of course, but they do so in different ways. These differences can sometimes become a source of tension in organizations, since the value created in one quadrant may be under-appreciated when viewed from the standpoint of another quadrant. For example, assume that we can map the percentage of human and financial resources dedicated to various functional activities in a typical manufacturing business. We might draw a map like the one in Figure 3.3, for example, to depict the production function in the organization. This map is created by showing a greater emphasis in a particular quadrant when a point on the diagonal line is drawn further away from the middle point. The further out on the line the point is drawn, the greater the degree of emphasis in that particular quadrant. (More will be said about how to precisely construct such a map or profile in Chapter 7.)

Typically, most of manufacturing's activities are in the Control quadrant. The focus is on improving costs, quality, and predictability. Some activities are devoted to maintaining employee morale and developing collaboration among employees – activities in the Collaborate quadrant – and some activities are devoted to understanding customer needs and helping the company

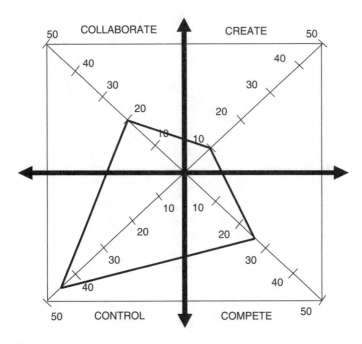

Figure 3.3   A map of the production function

increase competitiveness – activities in the Compete quadrant – but the Collaborate and Compete competencies' activities consume far fewer organizational resources than do those in the Control quadrant. Efficient procedures, mistake-free production, and on-time delivery are of central concern from the standpoint of the operations function.

From the standpoint of research and development or new product development, however, the preferred map would look quite different. Because the challenge is to create new products and services, stretch the boundaries of knowledge, and stay ahead of customer preference curves, these units require far more resources to be devoted to the Create quadrant. Figure 3.4 depicts a preferred resource map from the standpoint of R&D.

A typical new product development function requires that most of its resources be allocated to activities in the Create quadrant. This may involve new equipment, trial and error experiments, multiple prototypes, and an assumption of very inefficient processes. Some focus is typically dedicated to maintaining collaboration and teamwork among R&D staff members – the Collaborate quadrant – and constant contact is usually required with customers as well as monitoring the external environment – Compete quadrant activities – but little attention is paid to error-free, carefully controlled,

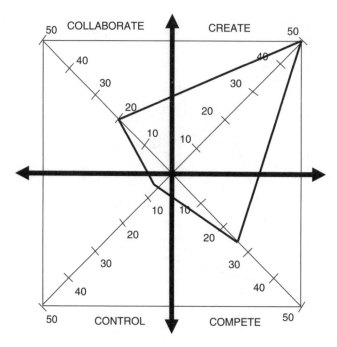

Figure 3.4   A map of the new product development function

tightly measured processes in the Control quadrant. Tension sometimes results in the typical company, therefore, when one function views resource allocation decisions from their own functional standpoint rather than from a company-wide perspective.

Similarly, the sales and marketing functions are continuously interacting with customers and clients, working hard to meet their needs, expectations, and time frames, and arguing for a product mix and service delivery process that creates customer loyalty. New products have to be better than those offered by competitors, and the name of the game is to outperform the competition. A map of this function's preferred resource allocation would typically look like Figure 3.5. Most company resources would be devoted to customers, generating rapid response, and activities that responded aggressively to external demands. Innovation and new product development are important to help respond to customers – the Create quadrant – and efficient and error free production is also a necessity – the Control quadrant. The slow, developmental approach typical of the Collaborate quadrant, however, is antithetical to the demands of the ever-changing marketplace, so few resources can afford to be allocated to those activities.

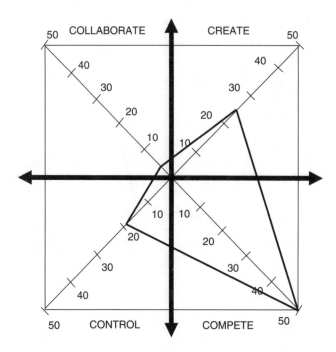

Figure 3.5   A map of the sales and marketing function

Finally, from the standpoint of the human resources and training and development functions, the most important resource allocation decisions that can be made are investments in human capital. Developing leaders, providing motivational incentives and compensation, and fostering employee engagement and loyalty are the keys to long-term company success. The preferred resource allocation map, therefore, typically looks like Figure 3.6. Opportunities for individual discretion and initiative are important – the Create quadrant – as are adequate measurement and appraisal systems – the Control quadrant – with a constant eye on the customer – the Compete quadrant – but empowerment, cooperation, teamwork, and human development get by far the highest allocation of resources.

The point is that each functional area in a typical company views its primary mission slightly differently, and resource allocation decisions always require tradeoffs and compromises. Any organization that ignores or devalues one function, for example, is likely to have a difficult time succeeding in the long run. External conditions and corporate strategies may dictate that some allocation priorities take precedence over others, of course, and organizational life cycles may also help determine when certain

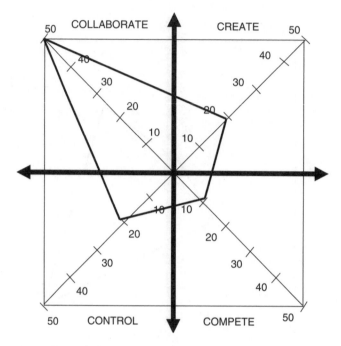

Figure 3.6   A map of the human resources function

functions are advantaged relative to others (Quinn and Cameron, 1983). Moreover, each functional area will prefer that resources be allocated to activities in all four competencies, but the relative allocation of resources will vary from one functional area to the next. Predictable tensions are likely to arise, therefore, and the Competing Values Framework can help firms diagnose appropriate trade-offs.

COMPETITION ACROSS QUADRANTS

An important insight highlighted by the Competing Values Framework, then, is that competing values, competing preferences, and competing priorities exist in any organization. Activities in the four quadrants compete for constrained resources. It is sometimes difficult to appreciate how they all create value when resource allocation priorities are viewed from different vantage points in the organization. It is even more difficult to understand how the seemingly competing values may become complementary values.

As has been emphasized before, the value-enhancing activities located in quadrants diagonally across from each other appear to be diametrically

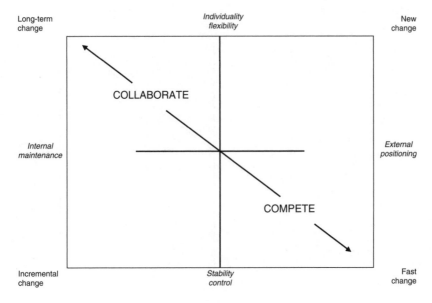

Figure 3.7   The Compete versus Collaborate quadrants

opposed. Thus, a person who works primarily in the Compete quadrant will typically view many activities in the Collaborate quadrant as actually destroying value (Figure 3.7). The reason for this is simple. People self-select in deciding the area of the organization in which they want to work and the kinds of value-creating activities in which they want to engage. Those who work in a functional area focused primarily in the Compete quadrant (e.g., strategic marketing) develop a deeply rooted belief that the best way to add value is by engaging in the activities associated with that particular quadrant. Further, the performance metrics with which they assess the value of any activity are those best suited for the activities in the Compete quadrant (e.g., sales, profits, customer returns). Viewed from the perspective of these metrics, much of what happens in the Collaborate quadrant looks like a waste of resources (e.g., training, team meetings, empowerment activities).

The same logic applies to the Control and Create competencies (see Figure 3.8). The low success rate and the unpredictability of project completion times that characterize the Create quadrant are abhorred by those whose focus is in the Control quadrant. The reason is that the Control quadrant prides itself on a high success rate and predictable project completion times. If those focused in the Control quadrant behaved like those focused in the Create quadrant, they would be considered failures.

Value creation

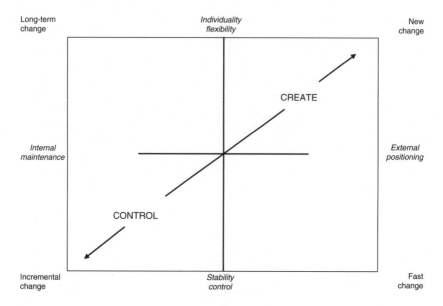

Figure 3.8   The Create versus Control quadrants

Because different functional areas in the organization assign differing degrees of importance to the different competencies, it is easy to see why they often work at cross-purposes. The vocabulary, mechanisms, priorities, required management skills, and measurement systems of the four competencies are so different that even if everybody in the organization is creating value, not everyone would recognize it or value it.

Because every organization faces constrained resources, allocating more assets to one quadrant will diminish the value creation potential of the quadrant diagonally across. Any move toward one quadrant will typically pull the organization away from the diagonally opposite quadrant. For example, the teambuilding and social capital development activities of the Collaborate quadrant create expenses that detract from value creation as measured by the Compete quadrant, where the metrics are quite often short-term, bottom-line, financial impact. Similarly, when a corporation responds to the call of the Compete quadrant and restructures itself by downsizing a portion of its workforce, those in the Collaborate quadrant see the decision as a reckless destruction of value for short-term gain. In their eyes, it disrupts the organization's culture and can damage employee morale.

Take Scott Paper Company as an example. The world's largest producer of consumer tissue products had performed poorly in financial terms for four years in a row, forcing the board of directors to bring in Albert Dunlap as chairman and CEO in 1994. Dunlap responded by substantially restructuring the company, adopting incentive-based compensation, and firing over 11 000 people. These were classic moves of someone operating in the Compete quadrant, moves that immediately generated substantial shareholder value. But, they came across as value destroyers to observers in the Collaborate quadrant because of the perceived destruction of human and social capital. The enemy, it is generally assumed, lives in the quadrant diagonally across from our perspective, and this perception engenders numerous frictions in organizations.

AS THE ORGANIZATION EVOLVES SO DOES THE RELATIVE IMPORTANCE OF EACH QUADRANT

Although tensions naturally arise in terms of how value-creating activities are viewed in the different competencies, virtually every organization needs to pursue activities in all four competencies. The relative emphases on the different competencies will depend on strategic priorities, life cycle development, and environmental conditions.

An example of the shifts in priorities associated with different quadrants, consider the development of Apple Computer Company (see Cameron and Quinn, 2006). Steven Jobs and Steven Wozniak invented the first personal computer in the garage of Jobs' parents' home, and Apple Computer Company was subsequently formed to produce personal computers. With mid-20s Jobs as CEO, employees were young, dynamic, unconstrained people who prided themselves in being free of policy manuals and rule books. The culture was characterized by a strong emphasis on entrepreneurship, innovation, and originality (Profile A in Figure 3.9). As is typical of most Create quadrant companies, a single entrepreneurial, charismatic leader was setting direction, and the company was flexible and free-wheeling. The press described the group as renegades and 'crazies.'

Within a few of years of incorporation, Apple established one of the most successful ventures ever experienced in the industry – the formation of a group of 'pirates,' dubbed the Macintosh Team. This team of selected employees was charged with developing a computer that people would want to purchase for use in their homes. Until then, computers were large, intimidating pieces of hardware that merely replaced slide rules for engineers and mathematicians. They filled entire rooms. They computed numbers. Few would have considered using one for personal or family applications. This small group of Apple Computer Company pirates, however, designed and developed the Macintosh Computer – a fun, approachable, all-in-one kind

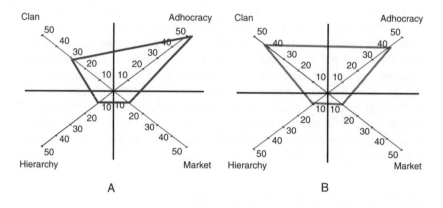

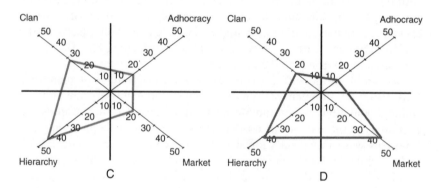

Figure 3.9 Change in emphasis in competing values quadrants over organization life cycles

of machine. It was the first to incorporate a mouse, icons or pictures on a screen, and software that could actually paint a picture (MacPaint) on what formerly had been only a computational device. This team's endeavors were so successful (as was the rest of the company's business) that the entire organization shifted priorities and culture. It came to look like Profile B in Figure 3.9 – a highly cohesive clan. Employees wore Apple logos on their clothes, had Apple bumper stickers on their cars, and spoke warmly of the 'Apple family.'

In a relatively short time, hundreds of thousands of Apple and Macintosh computers were being sold, distribution channels were expanding worldwide, and of a large array of highly competitive rivals emerged (e.g., IBM, Compaq, Wang). The freewheeling Apple clan was faced with a need for policies, standard procedures, and inventory controls. Rules and regulations were needed or, in other words, a Control orientation had to be developed (see Profile C). Apple's CEO, Jobs, was the quintessential innovator and team leader, perfectly comfortable in an organization where priorities were aimed squarely at the Create and Collaborate quadrants. He was not an efficiency expert and administrator and not inclined to manage in a hierarchy. John Scully from PepsiCo was hired, therefore, to manage the required shift in priorities toward stability and control.

Predictably this shift created such a crisis in the organization – with the former Collaborate and Create orientations being supplanted by a Control orientation – that founder Jobs was actually ousted from the company. The new set of values and priorities made Jobs' orientation out of sync with current demands. This shift to a Control orientation almost always produces a sense of exigency, of abandoning core values, of replacing family feelings with bureaucracy. John Scully was a master efficiency and marketing expert, however, and his skills matched more closely the shifting resource allocation priorities of Apple as its growth and expansion produced the need for this new orientation.

As Apple developed into a large, mature organization under Scully, a fourth shift occurred, as represented in Profile D in Figure 3.9. Apple ceased to be the agile, innovative company that characterized the young group of renegades in its early life, but instead was an outstanding example of efficiency and marketing proficiency. In many organizations, this profile becomes the norm, with the former Collaborate and Create resource allocation priorities being minimized and the Control and Compete priorities being emphasized. Many management consultants and leadership gurus almost exclusively focus on assisting companies to develop the capability to reinstitute team focused, collaborate, entrepreneurial, and flexible attributes. This is because many large and mature firms get stuck in their overemphasis on the Control and Compete quadrants. They lose sight of the importance of some resources being dedicated to the upper two quadrants. Such was the case with Apple, which narrowly escaped bankruptcy after 15 years of an overly restrictive emphasis on the two bottom quadrants. In the 1990s, Apple was saved from financial demise by the rehiring of founder Jobs who re-emphasized the company's priorities in the two upper quadrants.

Not that all four quadrants must be emphasized equally, of course, and not all effective firms have equal emphasis in each quadrant. Circumstances almost always dictate that an imbalance, in fact, is important. But, organizations must develop the capability to shift emphases when the demands of the competitive environment require it.

4. Tensions and trade-offs: from either/or to both/and thinking

In the previous chapters we have made the point that the Competing Values Framework introduces leaders to a new way of thinking. It highlights the tensions, tradeoffs, and conflicts that occur in almost all organizations, and it provides a way to diagnose and approach these tensions. Leaders must consider the competing values embedded in each of the four quadrants and identify appropriate tradeoffs in their strategic priorities and resource allocation decisions. Value creation occurs by effectively managing the tradeoffs highlighted by the four quadrants.

Another implication of the Competing Values Framework, however, is its ability to help leaders move from either/or thinking to a both/and thinking. That is, the framework can help leaders focus on the *integration* of competing values. In this way, apparently conflicting and opposing priorities are combined in ways that lead to the creation of value. This chapter elaborates the idea of both/and thinking in which leaders are encouraged to consider apparent opposing tensions and contradictions simultaneously. Finding the integration among divergent perspectives is the strategy being emphasized. We look first at the natural processes by which integration occurs in differentiated – or opposing – systems; then we discuss how the integration of opposites using both/and thinking can produce value in organizations.

REACTIONS TO UNCERTAINTY AND CHANGE

To illustrate the process of both/and thinking we will consider two science fiction movies about the same topic, the first encounter between the human race and beings from another realm. One movie was titled 'First Contact'. The second movie was titled 'Contact'. An examination of these two fictional movies may provide a metaphor for thinking about the integration of highly differentiated systems.

We begin with a question. What was the most important date in the history of the earth? The answer is 4 April 2063. According to the crew of the Starship Enterprise, this was the day of 'first contact'. It was the day that humankind first greeted an extraterrestrial civilization. Afterwards, nothing was the same. More value was created by that event than had been created by any event in the history of civilization.

In 'First Contact', the starship Enterprise leaves the twenty-fourth century as it pursues its evil enemy, Borg, back to the year 2063. This is a time just after World War III, in which much of the earth's population has been destroyed. It was on 4 April that Captain Zefram Cochran launched the first ship to travel at warp speed. At that very moment, a Vulcan ship was on a survey mission and was passing the Earth. The instruments on the Vulcan craft picked up the warp signature left by Cochran's foray into space. This signature told the Vulcans that Earth was a more sophisticated planet than they had assumed, and they decided to make contact with Earth.

The story recounts that the impact of first contact was astounding. The rules of value creation were radically changed. Technological progress was greatly accelerated. All of humankind became united in hope of a greater purpose and in the construction of a better universe. Poverty, sickness, and war were eliminated. Forever into the future, 4 April, 2063 was seen as the turning point in human history.

This story is being told from a historical perspective. It looks at the long-term effects of making contact with another world. In the second film, entitled 'Contact', a similar story is told but this time from a short-term perspective.

Ellie Arroway, played by Jodi Foster, was a young scientist obsessed with the notion of identifying communications from other planets. After considerable effort, she identified messages from external sources. The moment of contact occurred. The news created great uncertainty. Various groups began to demonstrate. Governments sought to protect their interests and came into conflict. Businesses began to pressure governments for strategic advantages. Conspiring scientists sought to steal credit and to take over the project. The national security agency and other government bodies began to interfere. In the short-run, this new condition was chaotic. People began to interpret and respond to the emerging rules of the new environment in unexpected ways.

Let us put these two striking story lines together. First, there is contact with an extraterrestrial system. As two dramatically different cultures come in contact with one another, confusion, tension, conflict, and spontaneous activity result. From the chaos, a new system emerges. The new system is highly differentiated – that is, there are two different cultures operating at once resulting in uncertainty and conflict. Eventually, the conflicts are worked out and a new more integrated system emerges. Assimilation occurs. The older system has been expanded in scope. It now has more variety in that it now includes the assets brought by the human race. The human system is elevated in terms of knowledge and capacity. It moves to a higher level of functioning.

These two movie accounts may help us think about the process of value creation. Breakthroughs in value creation frequently occur during a period in which two different systems meet. The integration of these systems may lead to a transformation, and new forms and capabilities may emerge.

The process is sometimes illustrated in natural settings, for example, as when an acorn falls into the soil and begins to draw moisture, warmth and nutrition. A transformation occurs and an oak tree begins to grow. The same can be seen in human biology. The male sperm and the female egg are distinct entities. Yet they, like the acorn and the soil, become joined in one interacting system. When they interpenetrate, new life begins. The integration of the two previously differentiated systems brings a transformation. Simple cells evolve into a more complex human body.

DIFFERENTIATION, INTEGRATION, INTERPENETRATION, AND TRANSFORMATION

Transformation means a change in the condition, nature, function, or form of something. Transformation usually involves a dramatic conversion, transmutation, or metamorphosis. The alteration may seem mysterious, magical, or even miraculous. People marvel, for example, that an oak tree can emerge from an acorn and the soil, or that a sperm and egg produce a human body. Yet, there are several predictable elements in this transformational process – differentiation, integration, interpenetration, and transformation.

'Differentiation' suggests that two systems exist which we interpret to be different and separate. The acorn is very dissimilar to the soil as the sperm is to the egg. 'Integration' means that the differentiated systems become connected. What was formerly unalike becomes a single entity. That is, 'interpenetration' occurs, in which one system becomes part of another system and a single, unified system results. What were formerly two systems becomes a single, unique system. The acorn becomes embedded in the soil, the shell cracks, and interpenetration occurs. The sperm and egg join and become one new system. In both instances, not only do the two systems become one system, but a 'transformation' occurs in which the new entity is not at all like either of the first two. The resulting oak tree, and the resulting human body, is not merely combinations of an acorn and soil or a sperm and an egg. The interpenetration has also created a transformational change in the entities. An entirely new biological system results.

These processes of differentiation, integration, interpenetration, and transformation are steps in nature's system of growth and development, but they also characterize the process of change in many aspects of human and organizational behavior. In particular, this process helps us understand the methods leaders frequently implement as they create entirely new value in organizations. Some illustrations will make this point clear.

JANUSIAN THINKING

Rothenberg (1979) analysed award-winning breakthroughs in fields such as music, science, art, and literature. He found a characteristic typical of all the breakthroughs. In each case, the initiator had what Rothenberg labeled a 'Janusian insight'. Janus is the Roman god depicted as having two faces pointing in opposite directions. A Janusian insight occurs when someone notices the simultaneous operation of two opposing ideas or concepts. Einstein, for example, said that the happiest thought of his life was when he conceived that an object could be simultaneously moving and at rest. He conceived of an event, for example, in which two objects are dropped from a high place. As they are falling, they are simultaneously moving and at rest, two opposing conditions that cannot exist at the same time. They are moving in relation to the ground but at rest relative to one another. The integration of opposites was the seed thought for Einstein's development of the theory of relativity. The integration of simultaneous opposite ideas led to an entirely new way to view the universe and natural phenomena – a transformation in physics. Similarly, in each breakthrough studied by Rothenberg, the initiator conceived of the integration of two opposing ideas.

COGNITIVE COMPLEXITY

The power associated with the process of integrating differentiated concepts can also be illustrated by examining the idea of cognitive complexity. Individuals who are deeply experienced in a particular activity have greater cognitive complexity about that activity than those who are novices. Cognitive complexity, in other words, refers to the degree of sophisticated understanding of a phenomenon that resides in a person's mind. Thus, a brain surgeon has greater cognitive complexity about the brain than does a dance instructor, while the dance instructor has greater cognitive complexity about rhythmic movement than does the brain surgeon. In each case, the experienced person is able to differentiate aspects of the phenomenon that the novice does not detect. Similarly, the experienced person is also able to integrate differentiated things in ways that the novice cannot.

Master musicians, for example, can both differentiate patterns of music and integrate them in highly creative ways. The classic concertos and sonatas of the world's greatest composers are examples of both differentiating themes and integrating themes in a single musical masterpiece. Cognitively complex managers can see the uniqueness and nuances embedded in a situation as well as the similarities and parallels, so that they are capable of pursuing a more advanced strategy in response. In sum, people with a greater capacity to differentiate and integrate concepts in a specific activity can add greater value to that activity than others not so experienced. Experience with interpenetration provides the potential to create transformational value creation.

LEADERSHIP

The processes of differentiation and integration are also typical of the research on leadership. The classic studies of leadership have found two key dimensions of leadership behavior – person-focused leadership and task-focused leadership (Bass and Stogdill, 1990). That is, this research uncovered the fact that some leaders tend to show concern for people (the soft side of leadership) whereas others tended to focus on getting things done (the hard side of leadership). However, by analysing decades of research on the effectiveness of these two leadership styles, researchers noted that the average correlation between the two orientations was statistically significant. That is, whereas leaders could be either task or person-focused, most effective leaders were both. They exhibited a capacity to integrate concern for people with concern for tasks, displaying soft characteristics as well as hard characteristics. Subsequent research has confirmed the superiority of the integration of these two orientations over an emphasis on either one singly. Integration trumps differentiation (Lawrence and Nohria, 2002).

What is remarkable is that very intelligent observers took years to notice the fact that effective leaders could be high on both orientations. They had held a differentiation perspective, and it was difficult to conceive of a both/and perspective. Hence, they failed to notice the interpenetration of opposites even though it was a central part of the phenomenon they were studying (Quinn, 2000).

ORGANIZATIONS

Another key finding in organizational studies is that more successful companies are more differentiated as well as more integrated than are less successful companies. For example, Lawrence and Lorsch (1967) introduced the idea that as organizations adapt to their environments over time, they tend to differentiate into more and more departments and subunits. These subunits take on unique characteristics in terms of their goals and purposes, the formality of their structures, the treatment of people, their subcultures, and their time orientation. As organizations become more differentiated, integration of these units becomes much more difficult. However, Lawrence and Lorsch found that the more successful companies were both more differentiated and more integrated than less successful companies. Successful firms integrated disparate units by means of common cultures, policies and procedures, organizational structures, an overriding vision, and other similar integrating mechanisms. Brown and Eisenhart (1997), in studies of organizations in Silicon Valley, confirmed the finding that organizations that were simultaneously characterized by greater differentiation and greater integration were better value creators than other organizations.

MANAGEMENT

We know a man who has spent the last 20 years building a family business. He is a creative leader with a knack for anticipating the technological future. Over the years he has made a number of risky decisions that positioned his company for significant growth. On the other hand, he is not the kind of manager who keeps all the details in place. To manage the growth opportunities, therefore, he decided to find a person to complement his strengths. He hired a woman to be president of his most important division. She is a hard driver and has a detail orientation – the opposite orientation to his. Her administration and efficiency orientation – coupled with his – have produced spectacular results. She delivers or exceeds financial goals quarter after quarter. Yet, our friend has a problem.

His brothers are also significant figures in the business. Each of them sees this woman as the antithesis of the organizational culture. The company has always been a place of innovation, caring, and stability. Her hard-driving, results-oriented focus does not sit well with the traditional culture. She rubs them the wrong way. They tend not to trust her, and they put enormous and continuous pressure on their brother to get rid of her. This tension is very disconcerting for him, and he finds the conflict between his brothers' demands and his division president's performance to be very painful. When asked why he continues to endure this tension, his answer was straightforward: 'Keeping her is best for the business.'

Of course, our friend does not see his decision in terms of differentiation and integration. Yet, that is one interpretation of what is going on. He has chosen to differentiate by hiring a woman as president who contradicts the normal expectations of others in the company. Her style tends to produce conflict, and these differentiated systems (the president's style, the brothers' preferences, the traditional culture of the firm) have a tendency to pull the system apart. The separation has not occurred, however, because of the decision by our friend to seek integration. The conflict causes him personal discomfort, but the organization excels because of it. His willingness to play an integrating role has led to more value being created than could have been produced without the integration of opposites.

INTEGRATION AND FINANCIAL PERFORMANCE

This point relating to the integration of opposites is a key point in the Competing Values Framework's approach to value creation. Our own research, described in Chapter 7, also confirms that superior financial performance is achieved by organizations that integrate the tensions and oppositions represented by the four quadrants of the Competing Values Framework. These findings indicate that the best value-creating firms in most industries integrate the differentiated dimensions of the four quadrants to a greater extent than do other organizations. A strategy of integration interpenetration becomes a pathway that effective leaders pursue as they seek to create new value in their organizations.

These examples from biology, cognitive processes leadership, organizations, and management each point out that people, relationships, organizations, and societies with the capacity to integrate their differentiated parts are likely to develop more new ideas, more new strategies, and more new value than those without those capabilities. In the story about our entrepreneurial friend, for example, a higher value was placed on the good of the company than on his own level of comfort. He was willing to experience personal uneasiness in exchange for collective progress. In most firms headed by less insightful and less sophisticated managers, chances are that the woman would be replaced. The company might then have become less conflictual but also less successful. In other words, integration and interpenetration almost never occur without some discomfort, and leaders must usually demonstrate courage and perseverance to achieve the value that can be achieved through these means. The Competing Values Framework helps to provide the insight and perspective that makes the costs of integration worth the investment.

COMPETING VALUES AND WORLD VIEWS

The trouble is, many leaders have not developed a sophisticated enough worldview that motivates them toward the integration of opposites.

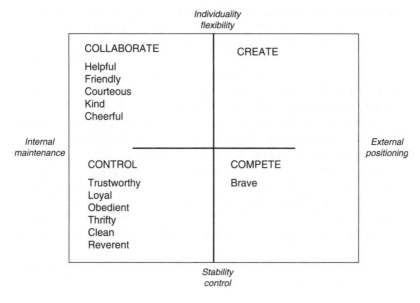

*Figure 4.1   The Boy Scout Law mapped on the Competing Values
Framework*

They maintain biases and thought processes that inhibit tensions and para-
doxes from surfacing. They resist taking into account opposing positive
values. To illustrate what we mean, consider an example of the American
Boy Scout movement (Quinn, 2000). A key tenant upon which the Boy Scout
organization is based is known as the Scout Law. Every Scout memorizes
this statement and seeks to live by it.

> A scout is trustworthy, loyal, helpful, friendly, courteous, kind, obedient, cheer-
> ful, thrifty, brave, clean, and reverent.

This statement reads like the description of the ideal boy. It is frequently
used as an illustration of the virtues to which every young man should aspire.
Yet is it really? If a boy fully embraced the Boy Scout Law, what would the
young man be like? We have used the Competing Values Framework to classify each of the 12 points indicated in the Boy Scout Law.

In constructing these attributes, the leaders of the Boy Scout movement
were no doubt reflecting their own core values. They most likely thought that
this list of valued attributes was very broad in scope and quite comprehensive. Yet, the Competing Values Framework points out that this is not the case
(Figure 4.1). The heretofore unexamined assumptions embedded in the

Scout Law suggest that an ideal boy is dependable and social. The Scout Law places little value on attributes of a boy related to self-assertion and innovativeness. There seems to be no value whatsoever on the notion of a boy who is creative, visionary, sees things in a different way, and seeks to explore unknown paths. Aggressive, commanding, and achievement-oriented young men are not described by this Law. A cynic might interpret the Scout Law as communicating that an ideal boy is one who stays within the boundaries defined by adult authority figures and is cheerful and friendly in the process. What is not included is a set of values that would prescribe a very different kind of young man. Perhaps these values explain a small part of the fact that the Boy Scout movement has had limited success with children in impoverished areas. Perhaps a boy in the ghetto knows that his survival depends less on compliance to authority than on the values in the two right quadrants of the Competing Values Framework. A Scout Law accounting for the opposite quadrants in the Competing Values Framework would read very differently:

> A scout is creative, independent, powerful, self-determining, challenging, strong, questioning, realistic, expansive, wise, engaged, and exuberant.

This analysis may seem like an analytic game, yet the point we are illustrating is an important one. We do not intend, of course, to denigrate the Boy Scout movement or the Boy Scout Law (which the authors all memorized as young men). Like the author of the Scout Law, we all do precisely the same thing when we are called upon to articulate our desired values, our desired future, or our preferences for creating value. We all create our own versions of the Scout Law. Initial attempts to create value are almost always one-sided and too narrow.

DENIGRATING OPPOSITES AND CYCLES OF CHANGE

In organizations, leaders reflect their assumptions and biases in almost every meeting and in every interaction. They assume desired futures that are simply reflections of their own worldviews. They articulate a desirable future that, unfortunately, tends to negate the values that are in opposition to their own worldview. If, for example, a leader values order and efficiency in the organization, he or she might say: 'We cannot afford to have any loose-cannons around here.' One implication of this statement is: 'We do not want anyone to take risks or display creative initiative in this organization.' Without realizing it, by defining initiative takers as 'loose-cannons,' a leader may unintentionally condemn empowered action and change. The reverse is also possible. Leaders may condemn order and deify change by saying something like: 'We can no longer afford to have bureaucrats around here. Everyone must be a change agent.' In making this statement, leaders are implicitly condemning control, order, and predictability.

Leaders may be deceived that they are creating major organizational change as they articulate a clear and unequivocal set of values that are one-sided. These major changes, however, are not the kinds that create new value. For example, a leader may notice that the organization is in need of more measurement, more efficiency, and more fine-tuning. Processes may be out of control. Consequently, the leader begins to denounce chaos and discuss the need for more centralized control. This leads to many discussions about how to reorganize in order to achieve the desired articulated values. Eventually there is a major reorganization. A new, more centralized structure is put in place. The leader is satisfied that value has been created. However, a short time later, it becomes clear that problems arise from the inflexibility, slowness of operations, and abundance of check-offs and procedures. The possibility of decentralizing begins to enter conversations. The leader condemns bureaucracy and advocates more flexibility and speed. Another reorganization is initiated, this time to decentralize, and the leader assumes that new value has been created. In reality, this swing of the pendulum from more or less centralization and control produces reorganization and change, but it seldom creates new value. Much energy and effort are spent in the process of reacting to an unbalanced and one-sided value set. Not taking into account the competing values in all four quadrants lead to vicious cycles of reorganization and change with little new value being created.

SCHISMOGENESIS

Gregory Bateson (2002) called this process 'schismogenesis' (the creation of schisms). Schismogenesis refers to propositions, theories, or perspectives that are broken, partial, or split (schismo) at the outset (genesis). In the case of our example of cyclical change above, one differentiated value is continually selected over its positive opposite. While this process is common, it has a downside. It usually blinds people to the presence of positive opposites and the possibility of integrating them. It frequently produces temporary success that will eventually turn into failure (without more cyclical change). The seeds of failure are planted at the outset of problem solving and value articulation.

Bateson was not the first to discover this phenomenon, of course. Many Eastern religious traditions recognize the dynamics of balance and imbalance in nature. Most of these perspectives espouse the need to avoid the stagnation and resulting stress that follow from separating seeming tensions. They call attention to the need to value and integrate opposites. They believed that the answer to a state of harmony and value creation is allowing opposing ideas to work simultaneously or by 'taking both sides at once.' In our terms, these Eastern religious philosophies simply point out that leaders create more value when they are Janusian, when they are both highly differentiated and highly integrated, and when they capitalize on interpenetration and transformation in their attempts to synergize. Rather than leading change that simply responds to the swing of a pendulum from one value set to another – i.e., from more control to less control – the Competing Values Framework helps leaders see how they can create new value and move beyond a reactive or reparative strategy. It allows leaders to do more than reorganize to repair the failures that arise from schizogenesis. One function of the Competing Values Framework, in other words, is to help leaders recognize what is missing in their visions and strategies, and to help identify the opposing values and perspectives that are necessary to achieve interpenetration and transformation.

AN EXAMPLE OF THE ENTREPRENEURIAL CYCLE

To illustrate this process in real organizations, consider the developmental history or almost any start-up you know. What we describe here is similar to almost all new entrepreneurial firms we have observed. A variation was described in the previous chapter in recounting Apple Computer's start-up, but it has been repeated in well-known firms such as Microsoft, Amazon.com, Hewlett-Packard, and even Ford Motor Company. Figure 4.2 illustrates the cycle of priorities.

The firm begins as a highly creative entrepreneur invents a new product or service and decides to build a company to produce and/or distribute it. Soon there are eight people working in an informal, tightly-knit team. They are filled with hope and enthusiasm. They work well together, interact frequently, and work hard. The primary goal is to grow the company, and they are very creative in their efforts. In competing values terms, the group is highly focused on Create quadrant activities with a moderate amount of emphasis in the Collaborate quadrant. Some attention is paid to Compete quadrant activities, but the Control quadrant seems to be of little relevance. In fact, the Control quadrant is usually defined negatively as an impediment to success (Plot A in Figure 4.2).

If the firm succeeds at this stage of development, a big jump usually occurs. The firm moves to an office building and hires additional staff. The workforce grows several-fold, but new problems begin to emerge. All these

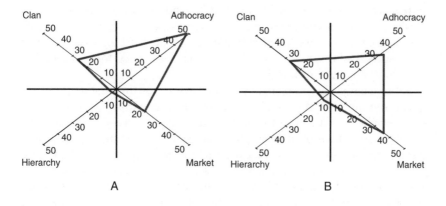

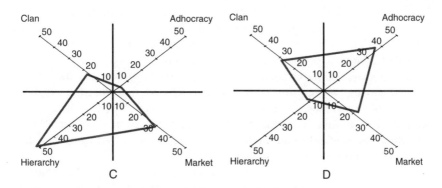

Figure 4.2 A common entrepreneurial company life cycle

people need coordination and management. Proposals are made to bring in more professional managers, better information systems, and more effective accounting tools.

The original cadre of founders – the original family – often resist. They condemn 'bureaucracy' and point out that available resources should be invested in the central goal, which is to grow. Often this is accompanied by a speech indicating how, since the early days of the company's history, the thing that made the company great has been its ability to respond creatively to challenges and to getting the job done against all obstacles. The entrepreneur pleads for integrity around the company's core values (which relate to creativity, risk, and growth). What often goes unnoticed is that the plea of the entrepreneur is split. Growth (positive) is being played-off against bureaucracy (negative) and organization, and the Control quadrant is viewed as an enemy to the firm's future success. Consequently, the organization continues to pursue growth and ignore the need for structure. The more successful it is at growing the more need is created for coordination and commitment (Plot B in Figure 4.2).

Subsequently, the problems associated with growth become more frequent and more intense. Because the founders have difficulty valuing the positive parts of the Control quadrant, they tend to emphasize with renewed fervor their original emphasis on the Create quadrant. Eventually an inversion occurs. The firm moves into a negative portion of the Create quadrant. It over-emphasizes the values of the Create quadrant and becomes a tumultuous anarchy void of the necessary stability and processes that ensure long-term survival. It produces less and less value, fails to make money, and is threatened with financial crisis.

Often at this point, the entrepreneur, the founder, or the parent figure, leaves the organization – voluntarily or involuntarily. It seems inconceivable that the founder would exit, but the founder's dream of building a creative, flexible, fast-growth company cannot be achieved using the current strategies. The company needs more 'management.' Consequently, more Control quadrant people are hired. The creative, entrepreneurial people begin to leave, and the company is saved by the control-oriented managers. Measurement, procedures, and systems replace free-wheeling, highly diverse efforts. Value increases, and the company celebrates its no-nonsense approach to productivity and efficiency. One can even hear conversations in which the original founding team is criticized for not knowing how to run a company (Plot C in Figure 4.2).

However, soon the organization begins to get stale. It begins to focus so much on carefully regulated systems that the values of the Control quadrant begin to be emphasized to an extreme. There is less capacity to adapt to the changing preferences of customers. If fact, customers' changing demands are sometimes seen as the enemy. The company begins to create less and less value as it develops into a frozen bureaucracy. If the firm survives, another revolution occurs, this time in reaction to the overly rigid hierarchical system that has developed. The opposite orientation – an entrepreneurial spirit – replaces the emphasis on stability and control (Plot D in Figure 4.2). Unfortunately, this cycle goes on and on.

Most managers and leaders in these entrepreneurial organizations tend to believe their situation is unique. They usually explain the entire process in terms of personalities – that is, the individuals involved were out-dated, incompetent, out of touch, naïve, or even malevolent. If they were to read these paragraphs they would be shocked to realize that someone unassociated with their situation could describe it so closely. Yet, what is actually happening is totally predictable. They are playing out a cycle that has gone on many times before. They cannot see it because they do not have the advantage of the Competing Values Framework. They have not integrated opposite leadership values and behaviors in a way that allows interpenetration to occur.

It is difficult to think about the integration of positive oppositions. Most people, most of the time, naturally condemn the opposing values. When the entrepreneur denigrates the values of the Control quadrant, he or she is usually doing it unconsciously. When the control-oriented employees criticize the risk-oriented entrepreneurs and visionaries in the firm, they do not understand that they are sowing the seeds of their own failure. Of course, this entrepreneurial cycle is just one example, but the point is that we all do things like this all the time. We destroy value because we are not naturally talented at simultaneously differentiating and integrating effectively. When the success of one set of values calls forth the need for the opposite positive values, we only see conflict and feel the need to fight or flee. We cannot imagine how to embrace and or integrate the oppositions and allow the conflict to propel us to a higher level of capacity.

The capacity to create value is determined at least to a certain degree by the amount of cognitive complexity that we carry. One advantage of the Competing Values Framework is to help people, at every level of the organization, consciously increase their cognitive complexity, to make them more Janusian, and to make them aware of the liabilities of either/or thinking. Creating both/and thinking is one of the key strategies that leads to value creation.

5. Creating value through new leadership behaviors

As we have asserted several times, the most successful organizations (and leaders) – those that create superior levels of value – tend to be simultaneously paradoxical. They are more differentiated as well as more integrated than their peer systems. They transform themselves by combining stability and flexibility along with internal and external perspectives, and, thereby they become Janusian in their orientation.

Of course, this kind of transformation is not the norm. Differentiated elements tend to remain separate. When they do come together, conflict and tension usually result because of an unconscious bias in almost everyone towards keeping dissimilar elements separate. Indeed, most people disconnect opposing elements by redefining them as discrete and unable to be integrated. They also tend to hold one set of values to be positive and uplifting while the opposite is defined as negative and diminishing. Leaders, therefore, must make a conscious effort to integrate contradictory factors and to manage the inevitable tension and resistance that accompanies such integration.

One function of the Competing Values Framework is to help leaders find ways to capitalize on the strengths of opposite quadrants and to think in ways that give rise to transformational thinking. In this chapter, we extend our discussion of both/and thinking and go one step deeper in analysing the implications of the framework for guiding transformational leader behavior. More specifically, the Competing Values Framework assists leaders in discovering a new pattern of thinking, a new language, and a new set of alternatives for value creation. This represents an even deeper level of understanding and application of the framework than was illustrated in previous chapters.

ADDRESSING NEGATIVE BIASES IN DIAGONAL QUADRANTS

Leaders who are strong in the Collaborate quadrant might be seen as patient, caring, selfless, authentic, sensitive, and principled. In the opposite

Compete quadrant, effective leaders might be seen as powerful, bold, challenging, assertive, connected, and task-involved. When these two leader types evaluate one another, however, they are less likely to focus on the positive attributes in the opposite quadrant. Rather, they tend to put a negative bias on these attributes. Collaborate quadrant leaders may see powerful, bold, challenging, assertive, connected, and task-involved as oppressive, overbearing, self-serving, corrupted, antagonistic, and cynical. Compete quadrant leaders may see patient, caring, selfless, authentic, sensitive, and principled as permissive, indulgent, lenient, detached, weak, and aloof.

Similarly, leaders who are strong in the Create quadrant might be visionary, optimistic, and enthusiastic. Because of an emphasis on discovery, these people might be adaptive, receptive, and willing to explore and learn. In the opposite quadrant, Control leaders might be seen as logical, realistic, and practical. These reliable and dependable people might be described as secure, assured, and consistent. However, if individuals whose strength lie in the Create quadrant are evaluating Control quadrant leaders, labels such as skeptical, inflexible, closed, and rigid are often used. Likewise, Control quadrant leaders who evaluate the attributes of Create quadrant leaders are apt to describe them as impractical, deluded, unrealistic, and even air headed. Negatively labeling opposite attributes is a predictable and understandable phenomenon. Good and bad, black and white, light and dark, normal and abnormal, effective and ineffective are common differentiators we impose to make sense of the complexity we experience around us. We create continua with each end labeled by an opposing or contradictory value.

Of course, most people are aware that opposites must be kept in balance or must be acknowledged as being part of existence. No person or organization is all one thing without also having attributes of the opposite. The need to accept the negative along with the positive is universally acknowledged. That is why almost everyone concedes that there can be no happiness without misery, no pleasure without pain, no good without evil, no light without dark. These good and bad conditions must be recognized and balanced.

The Competing Values Framework not only surfaces and highlights opposites, but it makes it possible to readily see the commonality in the apparent opposites. It extends beyond seeing only tension in opposing perspectives by guiding the integration of positive opposites. That is, the Competing Values Framework reminds us that even though diagonal quadrants are competing or conflicting, both values are desirable and both create positive value. Hence, highlighting and integrating positive opposites can produce a new kind of insight and value creation.

Value creation

A METHOD FOR CREATING NEW STRATEGIES AND NEW INSIGHTS

To be more specific, the Competing Values Framework can create an entirely new approach to leadership. It can enable leadership to reach a deeper, more transformational level. It does this by actually fashioning a new set of concepts by which leadership behavior can be guided. These new concepts integrate conflicting or opposing terms, but the integration is based on positive opposites instead of negative opposites.

To illustrate, consider two common but contradictory leadership actions: emphasizing teamwork and collaboration among employees compared to emphasizing speed and urgency. Teamwork activities take a fair amount of time, focus mainly on interpersonal relationships, and reside in the Collaborate quadrant. Emphasizing speed and urgency, however, requires rapid response, a focus on immediate outcomes, and they reside in the Compete quadrant. Usually leaders must tradeoff these two emphases – the more teamwork the less speed, and the more urgency the less collaboration. However, consider the process in Figure 5.1 that identifies a way to integrate the positive aspects of both leadership activities.

We have used boxes, labeled B and D, to list the two contradictory emphases. Both emphases could be pursued exclusively – to the detriment of the opposite emphasis – and either emphasis could be pursued to an extreme. When, for example, leaders overemphasize teamwork and collaboration, they may engender excessive discussion, unproductive partic-

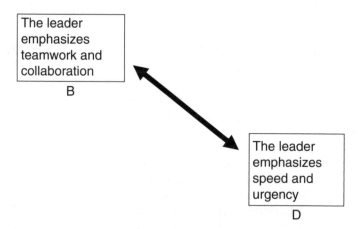

Figure 5.1 Two competing activities (the Collaborate and Compete quadrants)

ipation, and an inability to make a decision. Too much emphasis on involvement becomes a negative attribute. Similarly, too much emphasis on speed and urgency may produce tyrannical directives, defensiveness, and a loss of focus on long-term results. Excessive emphasis on any leadership activity typically produces a negative condition. The most common leadership mistake, however, is not so much an extreme emphasis on positive behaviors as it is the ignoring of the positive opposite behavior.

The extreme or exclusive forms of these leadership behaviors are listed in boxes A and E in Figure 5.2. That is, we can think of a continuum with the extreme negative behaviors anchoring the ends of the continuum.

Now consider what the middle box in the continuum might signify (Figure 5.3). It would identify a condition where the two contradictory emphases are not conflicting at all but are integrated. Opposing conditions are pursued simultaneously. This usually requires integrating concepts that were previously thought to be incompatible or incongruous. Box C illustrates the development of a new concept that may not have been considered previously, for example, speedy teamwork or urgent collaboration. Substituting synonyms for these concepts raises the possibility of leadership actions such as pursuing intense unity or rapid alliances. That is, the leader is cued to consider

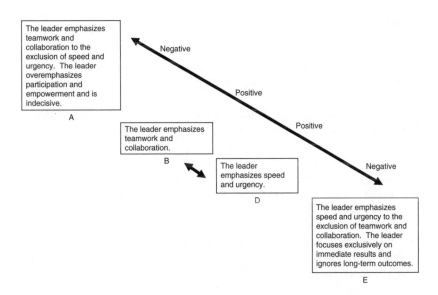

Figure 5.2   Two competing activities (anchored by extreme forms of leadership behaviors)

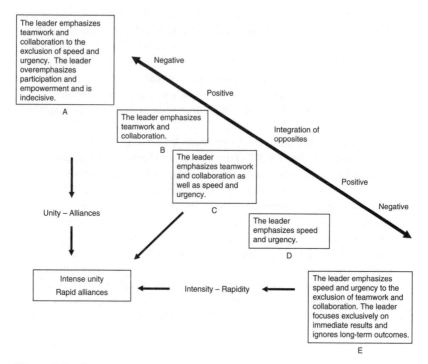

Figure 5.3   Integrating competing activities

behavior that integrates previously defined opposites. New possibilities are uncovered for creating value and for engaging in heretofore unconsidered leadership behaviors.

In the remainder of the chapter we discuss four new leadership behaviors that emerge from an integration of positive opposites using the Competing Values Framework. These behaviors are a product of the integration of leadership activities that are usually considered to be opposing and competing. The value of integrating these contradictory concepts is that leaders are able to identify new ways to create value – or to effectively perform their roles as leaders – that would not have been considered otherwise. Value creation takes a large step forward. The derivation of each new leadership behavior is illustrated in a figure, and then the four leadership behaviors are integrated into a single framework of unique value creating leadership. The four concepts being derived are: assured engagement, practical vision, teachable confidence, and caring confrontation.

LEADERSHIP BEHAVIOR #1: AUTONOMOUS ENGAGEMENT

'Autonomous engagement' is an example of a unique leadership behavior that integrates activities in the Compete quadrant and the Collaborate quadrant. It is derived from combining two positive values that are often in opposition. The first is autonomy (found in the Compete quadrant). The second is engagement (found in the Collaborate quadrant). To be autonomous as a leader is to be secure, self-determined, and self-reliant. It is to act independently or to feel that one is able to 'go it alone.' Individuality is valued. Some spiritual traditions indicate that to achieve a high degree of autonomy and individuality one should withdraw from the world – e.g., retreat to a convent, enter a monastery or engage in a 40-day fast. Hence, individuals achieve autonomy as they achieve independence from external pressures. They develop their own individuality. The potential problem, of course, is that extreme forms of autonomy lead to avoidance of others. In demonstrating independence, one may also demonstrate aloofness, withdrawal, or isolation – all negative manifestations of a positive attribute.

The opposite of avoidance is engagement. People who engage with others are involved, connected, and collaborating. They rely a great deal on social interaction with others. They emphasize high quality connections among people, and rely on human capital to produce value. Individuals who are too involved, of course, may lose perspective, self-direction, and integrity. They may become corrupted or compromised as they try to please the group. They become reliant on others to create standards and behavior patterns and lose sight of their own core values. These negative manifestations of a positive value tend to illustrate over-emphasis or exclusive emphasis on a positive leadership behavior.

In Figure 5.4 we show how the integration of these positive opposite behaviors leads to new insight about a type of leadership behavior that can produce extraordinary value. That is, leaders who engage in behavior characterized by the integration of these positive but opposite behaviors – for example, autonomous engagement, composed involvement, secure connectedness, and confident collaboration – create more value than would otherwise be possible. In spiritual traditions the challenge is expressed as 'being in the world but not of the world.' We refer to this condition as autonomous engagement because it integrates the notion of security and independence with the concept of involvement and togetherness. This concept, we will argue, is a key attribute of leaders who effectively create value.

Autonomous engagement represents an interpenetration of two positive, but usually differentiated, values. When leaders pursue an integration of these two values, they tend to become deeply involved with others but their

Value creation

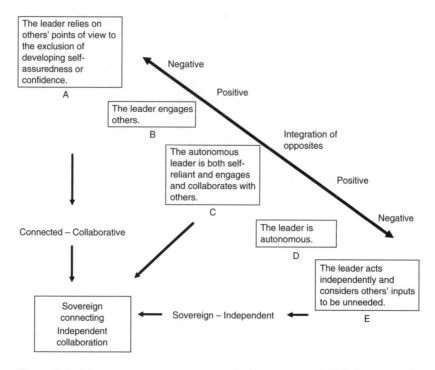

The leader relies on others' points of view to the exclusion of developing self-assuredness or confidence.

A

Negative

Positive

The leader engages others.

B

Integration of opposites

The autonomous leader is both self-reliant and engages and collaborates with others.

C

Positive

Negative

Connected – Collaborative

The leader is autonomous.

D

The leader acts independently and considers others' inputs to be unneeded.

Sovereign connecting Independent collaboration

Sovereign – Independent

E

Figure 5.4   Autonomous engagement – the integration of Collaborate and Compete leadership behaviors

involvement is based on confidence and self-reliance. They engage in inter-actions based on their own value principles, not because of external rewards or pressure from others. They are both independent and interdependent – that is, they are inner directed and other focused. Autonomous engagement helps leaders avoid either too little or too much reliance on self or on others. To illustrate, consider the following experience (Quinn, 2000: 62):

I remember a man – I'll call him Garret – who attended my Leading Change Course at the Executive Education Center at the University of Michigan Business School. He was a company president. During the first three days of the course, he said very little. On Thursday morning, he asked if we might have lunch together, and I agreed. Over lunch he told me that if he had attended my course any time in the last five years, he would have been wasting his time. He had successfully turned around two companies and felt he knew everything there was to know about leading change.

Today, he told me, he was now a lot more humble. There were five companies in his corporation. He had turned two of them around and was seen as the shining star among the presidents. He had earned the right to lead the largest company in the corporation. The current president of that largest company, however, still had 18 months left until his retirement. In the meantime, Garret had been asked to try his hand at one more turnaround. There was a company in the corporation that was considered hopeless. It had once commanded a large market share for its product. Today, it had only a small percent of the market and was still shrinking. Nobody believed this company could be turned around, so if Garret failed in his efforts, no one would hold it against him.

It had now been 12 months since he took on the challenge. He felt defeated. Everything that had worked for him before, everything his past had taught him, failed in the present situation. Morale was dismal. The numbers were dismal. The outlook for the future was dismal.

I asked Garret what he thought he would do next. On a paper napkin he listed his short-term objectives. He began to draw an organizational chart. He described the people in each of the senior positions and described the assignments and changes he was going to make in regard to each person on the chart. I found his answer unexciting. There was no commitment or passion in what he was telling me. Yet it was clear that Garret was a man of character with a sincere desire to succeed. I took a deep breath and asked a hard question.

'What would happen if you went back and told those people the truth? Suppose you told them that you have been assigned as a caretaker for a year and a half. No one believes the company can succeed and no one really expects you to succeed. You have been promised the presidency of the largest company, and the plan is to put you into the plum job. Tell them that you have, however, made a fundamental choice. You have decided to give up that plum job. Instead, you are going to stay with them. You are going to bet your career on them and you invite them to commit all the energy and good will they can muster into making the company succeed.'

I was worried that I'd offended Garret. I half expected an angry response. He looked at me for a moment, and then it was his turn to take a deep breath. To my surprise and relief, he said, 'That is pretty much what I have been thinking.' He paused, and in that moment I watched him make the fundamental decision. Almost immediately, he picked up the napkin and started redrawing his plans. He said, 'If I am going to stay, then this person will have to go; this person will have to be moved over here; and this person . . .'

As he talked, there was now an air of excitement in Garret's words. Once he had made the fundamental decision to stay, everything changed. His earlier plans to move on to the larger company were suddenly scrapped. Garret had made a fundamental choice, and now he had a new life stance, a new outlook and a new way to behave. The organization chart that made sense a few moments before now made no sense at all. None of the original problems had changed but Garret had and this made all the difference in the world.

When leaders act with autonomous engagement, they actively seek involvement, but with a secure and well-grounded motive. They become deeply engaged in an activity based on their own sense of rightness and goodness, not based on the rewards it brings or the demands that others may exert. They seek involvement because it is the right thing to be doing at the moment. They are driven not externally but internally. They are neither self-absorbed nor dependent, but instead they are securely interdependent.

LEADERSHIP BEHAVIOR #2: PRACTICAL VISION

Another paradoxical leadership behavior that can emerge from the integration of two positive opposites in the Competing Values Framework is 'practical vision'. This behavior is based on the concepts of hope and vision (found in the Create quadrant) and the concepts of reason and practicality (located in the Control quadrant). Hope is associated with orientations such as optimism and faith. Vision is a natural companion to hope. People who are hopeful adopt a positive, enthusiastic orientation to life and they tend to see possibilities rather than problems. They develop visions and dreams of the future. Such people often radiate a positive influence that attracts and uplifts others. They see opportunities and potential instead of obstacles and blockages.

Hopefulness and vision are oft-cited attributes of effective leaders. They refer to leaders' responsibilities to envision the future, communicate dreams, and mobilize others to imagine positive outcomes. Visionaries and imaginative thinkers are highly prized in our fast-changing world. Those who can foresee the future and communicate vision are frequently heroically portrayed. Optimism and hopefulness are contagious, so these kinds of leaders tend to be described as charismatic and energizing.

Hope and vision, however, can also be negative. Individuals who overemphasize, or exclusively emphasize, these orientations can become impractical, deluded, and unrealistic. Leaders' hopefulness and their visions can be irrational, illogical, and unsound. They may be enthusiastic about things that are not realistic or that may even be harmful over time. They may ignore hard facts, practical advice, or reasonable perspectives. Visionaries are often seen as impractical, of course, so being so labeled is not always viewed despairingly.

The opposing positive attributes are reason and practicality (located in the Control quadrant). Reasonable people are logical, realistic, and rational. Such a person tends to look for facts, data, and what is known and certain. These kinds of leaders are described as grounded and sensible. Their practicality is often seen as evidence of wisdom and commonsense. They tend to focus less on unknown possibilities and more on experience and present realities. When practical leaders hear an account or an explanation, they ask, 'Is this logical, reasonable, and sensible?' They question things and want to see evidence. They are often orderly and systematic in their analyses.

Taken too far, of course, an over-emphasis or exclusive emphasis on reason and practicality can be negative. Leaders may become so focused on facts and data that they do not entertain experimental possibilities. They may emphasize order to the extent that they become stagnant, so wedded to logic that they become illogical, so pragmatic that they become skeptical of all unproven possibilities. An exclusive reliance on rationality and pragmatism ensures a reactive, non-vibrant, even boring existence.

The Competing Values Framework suggests how the integration of these two opposites can be a key to effective leadership. Achieving practical vision is a product of combining hope, faith, and optimism with reason, logic, and practicality, as illustrated in Figure 5.5. Such integration lies at the heart of creativity and breakthrough thinking. Studies of creativity, for example, suggest that great insights are often a product of intense logical preparation coupled with vision of something previously unknown (Cameron, 2005a; DeGraff and Lawrence, 2002). The practicality of preparation coupled with the hopefulness of imagination have often led to major breakthroughs (Rothenberg, 1979). Intuition and insight tend to occur in people who have exercised both faith and common sense.

Leaders who develop practical vision can see both the realities and practicalities of the present situation as well as the possibilities and prospects that may exist in the imagined future. They have an appreciation and a

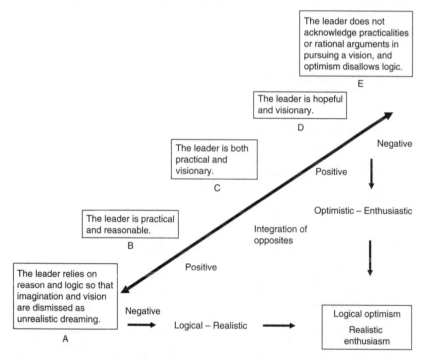

Figure 5.5   Practical vision – the integration of Control and Create leadership behaviors

reverence for both reality and potential. We can see a better future and can explain it in a reasoned way that reaches people at both logical and intuitive levels. Others resonate with the leader's vision because it is both logically and emotionally true.

This notion of practical vision is often captured in the parables of Eastern thought. In one such parable, 'The sound of the forest,' a prince goes to a great master to learn how to become a leader. The master sends him to study the sound of a forest. A year later the prince returns to report on the sounds made by the wind in the trees and the songs of the birds. The disappointed master sends the prince back to hear more. The discouraged prince returned to the forest and for days hears only what he had heard before. Then, gradually, he starts to become aware of faint sounds, and he listens to them more carefully. The sounds gradually became clearer, until he starts to experience the forest in a new way. He returns to the master and describes the sounds of the flowers opening, the sun warming the earth, and the grass absorbing the dew. The delighted master responds: 'To hear the unheard is necessary to be a good leader.'

This principle is similar to a classic article written decades ago regarding the prescriptions for personal fulfillment. It describes a person who visited his physician as a result of depression, loss of energy, and general malaise (Gordon, 1959).

> He told me to drive to the beach alone the following morning, arriving not later than nine o'clock. I could take some lunch; but I was not to read, write, listen to the radio, or talk to anyone. 'In addition,' he said, 'I'll give you a prescription to be taken every three hours.'
>
> He then tore off four prescription blanks, wrote a few words on each, folded them, numbered them, and handed them to me. 'Take these at nine, 12, three, and six.'
>
> 'Are you serious?' I asked.
>
> He gave a short bark of laughter. 'You won't think I'm joking when you get my bill!'
>
> The next morning, with little faith, I drove to the beach. It was lonely, all right. A northeaster was blowing; the sea looked gray and angry. I sat in the car, the whole day stretching emptily before me. Then I took out the first of the folded slips of paper. On it was written: LISTEN CAREFULLY.
>
> I stared at the two words. 'Why,' I thought, 'the man must be mad.' He had ruled out music and newscasts and human conversation. What else was there?
>
> I raised my head and I did listen. There were no sounds but the steady roar of the sea, the creaking cry of a gull, the drone of some aircraft high overhead. All these sounds were familiar.
>
> I got out of the car. A gust of wind slammed the door with a sudden clap of sound. 'Am I supposed to listen carefully to things like that?' I asked myself.
>
> I climbed a dune and looked out over the deserted beach. Here the sea bellowed so loudly that all other sounds were lost. And yet, I thought suddenly, there must be sounds beneath sounds – the soft rasp of drifting sand, the tiny

wind-whisperings in the dune grasses – if the listener got close enough to hear them.

On an impulse I ducked down and, feeling fairly ridiculous, thrust my head into a clump of sea-oats. Here I made a discovery: If you listen intently, there is a fractional moment in which everything seems to pause, wait. In that instant of stillness, the racing thoughts halt. For a moment, when you truly listen for something outside yourself, you have to silence the clamorous voices within. The mind rests.

I went back to the car and slid behind the wheel. LISTEN CAREFULLY. As I listened again to the deep growl of the sea, I found myself thinking about the white-fanged fury of its storms.

I thought of the lessons it had taught us as children. A certain amount of patience: you can't hurry the tides. A great deal of respect: the sea does not suffer fools gladly. An awareness of the vast and mysterious interdependence of things: wind and tide and current, calm and squall and hurricane, all combining to determine the paths of the birds above and the fish below. And the cleanness of it all, with every beach swept twice a day by the great broom of the sea.

Sitting there, I realized I was thinking of things bigger than myself – and there was relief in that.

What is the principle that lies at the foundation of the master's wisdom? Why does leadership require hearing the unheard? One answer is that leadership requires both an understanding of deep structure – the elements in the forest or the beach – as well as the unfolding potential of the system – the sounds beneath the sounds. Leaders understand both realities and the possibilities. They can both differentiate these elements and see the possibilities in their integration. Their vision is informed by both observable elements and imaginary possibilities. Their logic accounts for both elements that are impractical as well as observable data.

In summary, effective leaders combine hope and reason. They strive to be hopeful and logical, visionary and realistic, enthusiastic and practical. Practical vision means that they have a deep understanding of present reality. They see deeply into the system that exists while having a reverence for the potential that lies within the system. They can explain what is and what might be in a reasoned way. Others resonate with their practical vision because it is both factually and emotionally true.

LEADERSHIP BEHAVIOR #3: TEACHABLE CONFIDENCE

A third leadership attribute stimulated by the use of the Competing Values Framework is an interpenetration of confidence, security, or assuredness (Control quadrant attributes) and humility, openness, or teachableness (Create quadrant attributes). Confident leaders have a belief in themselves. They are certain that they have all the capability they need to perform a given task. They are secure, centered, and self-assured. They have a sense of self-efficacy – a prerequisite for high performance in any human being (Bandura, 1997). Self-efficacy means that individuals have a sense of competence and ability to successfully accomplish the task being faced. Moreover, they are inherently optimistic. It is difficult to imagine a leader who does not have the confidence to step out, to provide direction and vision, and to endure disagreement and adversity. Confidence, assuredness, and self-efficacy are among the attributes most people find attractive in a leader.

Of course, it is also possible for leaders to be too confident, or to be confident to the exclusion of openness. They can become proud and suffer from hubris, conceit, or arrogance. They can rely too much on their own capabilities and knowledge. They can interpret the support they receive and the accolades that accompany their leadership roles as evidence that they do not need others' inputs. Unfortunately, it is not unusual for leaders to develop over-inflated opinions of themselves and lose the capacity to learn from others. Such leaders, over time, become rigid, conceited, and vain. They may even become disconnected from reality and vulnerable to losing touch with emerging change or progress.

The positive opposite of self-confidence and assuredness is humility, openness, or teachableness. Humility does not imply weakness or lack of personal strength. It is, rather, an awareness of one's own shortcomings. A humble leader is modest and receptive. Such a person tends to be receptive, approachable, and teachable. Humility in leaders helps them stay receptive to new information from many sources, to points of view that may not agree with theirs, and to opportunities that they did not think of themselves. Teachableness leads to listening, learning, and inquiring. A study by Jim Collins (2000) suggested that the key attribute of the most successful CEOs in the most successful organizations over the previous 40 years has been humility.

The virtue of humility, of course, can be taken too far. Humility can become the weakness of the self-effacing, self-denigrating leader who is filled with insecurity and fear. An insecure leader can be filled with anxiety and can be apprehensive, weak, undependable, and unreliable. Such a leader is seldom self-reliant, confident, and able to take initiative. Being too teachable can substitute for having a firm opinion or point of view, or it can block firm decision making. An over reliance on teachableness leads to wishy-washy stances, an absence of clear direction, and underdeveloped core values.

Coupling these two positive opposites – humility and self-assuredness – suggests that an effective leader should develop the capacity to display 'teachable confidence' (see Figure 5.6). A leader who practices teachable confidence is both responsive and centered, open and assured, receptive

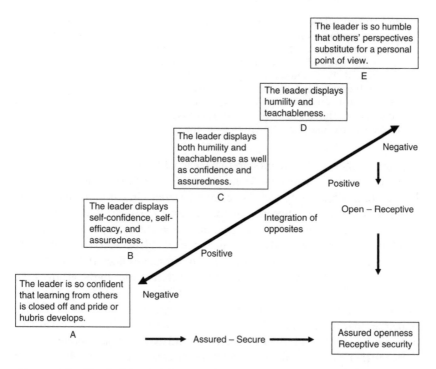

Figure 5.6   Teachable confidence – the integration of Control and Create leadership behaviors

and secure. The value that is created extends beyond what either the confident leader or the humble leader could provide without the presence of the positive opposite.

Teachable confidence is the capacity to face the unknown and to continually move forward so as to co-create a new reality. It is similar to the process of improvisation practiced by jazz musicians. The confidence exists in one's own abilities, but the necessity of staying attuned to others is the key to making beautiful music. The more confidence is coupled with teachableness, the more likely the outcome will be extraordinary. Similarly, leaders' teachable confidence can create value in unusual, complex, or changing situations, taking initiative, remaining open to feedback, learning from forays and even failures, and capitalizing on what is being learned. The leader is simultaneously stable and changing.

C. Terry Warner (2001) described an event in which this principle of teachable confidence was violated by a leader. The leader in this case was simply the host of a party in his own home.

Once during a New Year's Eve party in our home most of those present took turns letting themselves be coached in singing by one of the guests who was a professional voice teacher. Despite widespread urging, I declined. I said that I'd be too embarrassed. The jovial atmosphere seemed to vacate the room. After a bit, a few of the couples said they thought they should get home, and it wasn't even midnight. Only later did I realize that I was, in effect, saying to everyone present that I couldn't trust them enough to sing in front of them – they would judge me too harshly if I tried. My silent criticism of them made them feel uncomfortable, and they wanted to go home. (Warner, 2001, p. 67)

Being neither confident enough to be teachable, nor teachable enough to become confident, Warner's friend destroyed the positive energy of the group. He lost his ability to be an effective leader almost immediately. His guests wanted to leave because of the negative messages that he unintentionally sent by his inability to merge the two positive opposite attributes. Confidence is attractive and powerful, and teachableness possesses the same attributes. The absence of both produces the opposite effect. It dissipates the positive energy in individuals – or the power that resides in the group. Like a black hole, the light and energy is sucked out of the room by leaders who are confident without being teachable, teachable without being confident, or neither teachable nor confident. The interpenetration of these two attributes, on the other hand, frees the leader to add extraordinary value.

In another example, Bill Torbert (1987) discussed a concept very similar to our teachable confidence – his term was 'unconditional confidence.' He described unconditional confidence as the capability to discard inaccurate assumptions and ineffective strategies in the midst of ongoing action. Effective leaders, he asserted, are confident enough to act and humble enough to learn at the same time. Acting and learning, however, are not random events. They are guided, according to Torbert, by authenticity, or an adherence to internalized principles. When leaders' confidence is based on a consistent set of principles, when behavior matches those principles, and when learning helps refine, enrich, and mature those principles, the effectiveness of the leader increases.

Of course, everyone displays inconsistencies in behavior and violations of internal principles. Often those inconsistencies are labeled hypocrisy or lack of integrity. Leaders who integrate confidence and teachableness, however, are less likely to be so accused. Confidence based on internalized principles provides a substantial degree of stability in behavior. Moreover, teachableness provides a way for repentance and correction to occur, so observers are not given the impression that hypocrisy or integrity are at stake. Leaders characterized by teachable confidence simply have more influence, and can create more value, than they could without this integration of positive opposite characteristics.

One especially notable example is a former high school basketball coach in Ann Arbor, Michigan, named Brian Townsend. As a former professional football player, Brian was hired as the basketball coach to turn around a struggling program. It was clear from the outset that Townsend was confident but that he was willing to accept input. In his second year the team won the state championship, and the third year the team won the regional and district championships. Despite his success, Townsend had one particularly outspoken critic who adamantly opposed his hiring. Following Townsend's appointment, the critic worked hard to negate the value of Townsend's contribution, sometimes in the public eye. Townsend's demonstration of teachable confidence was most clearly seen in his reaction to this critic. When interviewed about this individual, Townsend replied:

> Why should I react to that? My team just won the state championship. These kids now believe in themselves and in the program. That is why I am here. That outweighs any criticism. The key is that we did it, not that I get the credit. If I can get the result I want for my team, I am perfectly willing to endure people who want to deny me that credit. It just does not matter.

LEADERSHIP BEHAVIOR #4: CARING CONFRONTATION

Caring confrontation is a concept that emerges from an interpenetration of two more positive opposites. The first is personal caring and concern (Collaborate quadrant attributes). Caring leaders demonstrate patience, support, and compassion. They are not self-focused but other-focused. Their intention is to help others grow and develop, to experience joy, and to flourish in their roles and responsibilities. They express concern by empathizing with the experiences of those with whom they work and by serving them selflessly. Such leaders can even be said to love their followers, a term used rarely in most organizational settings. This love is genuine, however, and stems from a deep commitment to the welfare of others. There is a serious commitment to the notion that human beings are the most important resource in any organization. Hence, caring and concerned leaders give a significant amount of emphasis to helping their people grow and flourish.

An over-emphasis or exclusive emphasis on caring and concern, of course, can become distorted and dysfunctional for both leaders and followers. Leaders can become permissive, indulgent, and lenient. They can remove responsibility and accountability from others by protecting them from the realities of organization expectations. They can compromise standards and become wishy-washy in upholding requirements. In such cases, leaders allow others to perform below their level of capability. Whereas this may be done in the name of personal concern or even love, the consequences are anything but loving and encouraging. Personal caring becomes debilitating. Co-dependence is a common consequence.

The positive opposite of caring and concern is *confrontation and challenge* (Compete quadrant attributes). These leaders are powerful, brave, and challenging. They see what needs to be done and boldly challenge others to do it. They are strong leaders who take action quickly and demand execution. They are exacting and hold high standards of performance. Some of the greatest leaders who ever lived have been described in this way – Napoleon, Patton, Alexander, Roosevelt, King. These leaders are unlikely to tolerate preventable errors, mediocrity, or laxity. Most observers suggest that Jack Welch, labeled as the greatest CEO of the twentieth century, was the quintessential confrontational and assertive leader. Shareholder value in General Electric improved more than 800 percent under his tutelage.

Taken too far, of course, confrontation becomes oppression. Commanding and demanding leaders can become overbearing, manipulative, and self-serving. They can create defensiveness in others by being too tough, too insistent, too intense, or too severe. We see this illustrated by some athletic coaches, military officers, or managers charged with downsizing or increasing efficiencies. Some see assertiveness as the only alternative to managing a difficult situation, so intimidation, punishment, or excessive requirements are meted out as standard fare. People respond by behaving differently when leaders are present than when they are not. People create protective mechanisms to minimize the personal pain or embarrassment engendered by these leaders. Sabotage and resistance are not unusual responses. Rather than producing positive effects and performance that meets high expectations, performance almost always declines (Cameron, 1998).

The desired characteristic of effective leaders, of course, is to be both caring and confrontational – some might call it tough love. That is, leaders who practice 'caring confrontation' are patient and powerful, compassionate and bold, selfless and challenging. They have the inclination to put the welfare of others ahead of their personal interests while boldly and unwaveringly challenging them to live up to a standard that is being modeled for them by the leaders themselves. Figure 5.7 represents these integrated behaviors.

Dutton et al. (2002) described a special example of leadership exhibiting caring confrontation in the University of Michigan Business School. It was demonstrated by former dean Joseph White when faced with an unusual event. An apartment building near campus caught fire and burned to the ground, destroying all the belongings of three business school students in the middle of the semester. The fire occurred on the eve of the dean's 'State of the School' address in which he reported on fund raising, enrollments,

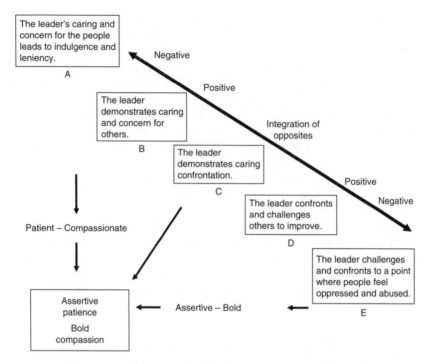

Figure 5.7 Caring confrontation – the integration of Collaborate and Compete leadership behaviors

academic achievements, research productivity, grants acquired, scholarly impact, and so on. In the business of business school leadership, such speeches have significant impact and are often noted by publications that rank business schools. The dean's approach to such occasions was traditionally no-nonsense, straightforward reporting, and it was typified by the highest standards of quality and precision. After learning of the disastrous events of the night before, however, the dean set aside his speech and turned the forum into an explanation of the event and a call for compassionate assistance. He took a check from his wallet and, in front of an audience of several hundred, wrote a personal check for $300 to help allay the students' expenses. The impact of that event, and the caring confrontation that he exemplified, resulted in an incredible mobilization of a similar amount of compassion, caring, and bold action on the part of the business school community. The caring was integrated in a very effective way with the usual rigorous standards and challenging culture that characterized everyday life on campus. Students reproduced class notes and computer files so that the students could continue with their studies. Accountability for maintaining the academic requirements were not dismissed. Rather, the victimized students were just assisted in maintaining the highest standards of excellent performance characteristic of the culture of the school.

This kind of response to caring confrontation occurs in almost every organizational setting, even in those least likely to be tolerant of words like love, caring, and affection. People respond to people who practice kindness and compassion, but they also desire straight shooting, telling it like it is, challenging mediocrity and non-excellence. This is illustrated by a conversation with a student who played football for Bo Schembechler, the charismatic former coach at the University of Michigan. The young man was a lineman that you wouldn't want to meet in a dark alley – tall, heavy, bulging at the seams, and eager to flatten the opposing quarterback. We asked him what he thought of Bo. He replied, 'Bo is the only person in the world that I will let kick me in the butt.' 'Why?' we asked. 'Because I know he loves me.' Tough football players don't usually use words like love to describe their butt-kicking coaches. They are taught to expect authoritative discipline from coaches on the football field. No one thinks of it as a place of love. Especially, big, tough linemen are not expected to use the L-word. Yet he did. He even implies that it is the love that makes the confrontation acceptable.

THE COMPETING VALUES FRAMEWORK AS A CREATOR OF NEW LEADERSHIP BEHAVIORS

We have provided four new concepts that exemplify effective leadership – concepts that help leaders create new value and enhance the effectiveness of their own and their organization's effectiveness. These four behaviors are not the usual fare in leadership descriptions. Most lists of leadership attributes and behaviors ignore the inherent contradictions in effective leaders' repertoires. They identify straightforward positive attributes and behaviors that are often incomplete. Leadership prescriptions often suggest only one aspect of a more complex set of paradoxical leadership attributes – i.e., leaders should be caring (not confrontational), visionary (not pragmatic), confident (not humble), engaging (not autonomous). The Competing Values Framework helps highlight the need for a deeper and more complex view of effective leadership. The leadership behaviors identified in this chapter arise through the integration of positive opposite concepts. These positive opposites are brought to mind by highlighting the tensions inherent in the diagonal quadrants of the framework. Emphasizing positive, not just negative, opposites leads to a new way to think about leadership.

Of course, many other concepts could have been developed in this chapter. We selected four simply because they represent the four quadrants

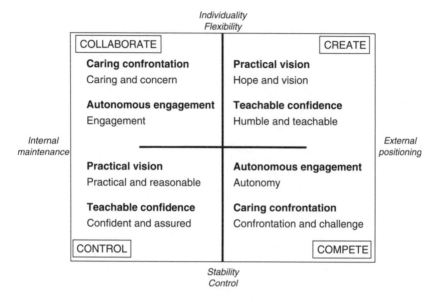

Figure 5.8   New leadership behaviors for creating value

in the framework. Figure 5.8 identifies the relationships of each of these concepts in the Competing Values Framework.

Our past research suggests that effective leaders behave in a way that is congruent with the culture of the organization in which they operate (Cameron and Quinn, 2006). Leaders who are caring, team oriented, and collaborative, for example, are likely to perform best in an organization's culture that emphasizes the Create quadrant culture. Similarly, a competitive, confronting, demanding leader tends to perform best in an organization in which the culture is dominated by the Compete quadrant. What this chapter points out, however, is that the most effective leaders – those that create the most value, or those that excel beyond the norm – are more complex than that. They are not only able to demonstrate competencies that are compatible with a congruent culture, but they add more value than their counterparts by integrating the opposite orientation as well. They are more cognitively and behaviorally complex. They achieve more value by bringing about both balance and improvement in opposite quadrants. They serve as leaders that provide value to their organizations that is seldom even recognized by others who do not reach this level of complexity. Thus, at this deeper level, the Competing Values Framework becomes a sophisticated tool to be used by leaders who rise above the ordinary and mundane.

PART II

Techniques for application

6. Predicting value creation and financial performance

The first five chapters of this book provided a view of how the Competing Values Framework helps leaders create value by expanding and enhancing an understanding of tradeoffs, tensions, possible integrations, and new leadership activities. We explained three different levels of analysis that the Competing Values Framework helps to highlight:

1. the importance of considering the competing and contradictory elements in leadership and in organizations that are necessary for effective performance;
2. the integration of opposites to create 'both/and' thinking in the pursuit of value creation; and
3. the creation of completely new and more complex strategies for leadership based on the merger of positive opposite terms.

In this chapter, we explain an important application of the Competing Values Framework. This application relates to predicting and enhancing the *financial* value of organizations (Thakor, 2001). That is, in addition to being useful for guiding leader behaviors, the Competing Values Framework also serves as a method for measuring and predicting financial performance. The framework does so at a level of accuracy that exceeds other such measurement frameworks (e.g., the Balanced Scorecard, Economic Value Added, and so on). Statistical analyses reveals that the rankings assigned to firms based on the Competing Values Framework display a contemporaneous correlation of about 74 percent with the market-value-to-book-value ratios of these firms. Thus, the Competing Values Framework correlates more highly with stock market valuation than other measures of which we are aware.

PRINCIPLES OF VALUE CREATION

To explain the power of the Competing Values Framework in predicting financial performance, we first review some basic principles of value creation and value creation strategy, and we borrow two concepts from economics – concavity and convexity. Whereas value creation is an inherently dynamic process and optimal rules are constantly evolving, two basic conditions can be identified that highlight fundamental principles of value creation: (1) a condition when the rules of value creation are known and defined clearly, and, (2) a condition when change is dynamic, unpredictable, and rules of value creation are being formulated in real time. The time horizon for judging value creation is very different across these two conditions. In the first condition, value creation is judged on the basis of well-defined metrics over relatively short time horizons. In the second condition, value creation is judged on the basis of evolving and imperfectly understood metrics over relatively long time horizons.

Many of the strategies used in the pursuit of value creation under changing and ambiguous conditions (i.e., the second condition above) will seem like value destruction if they are judged by the metrics of value creation under conditions where the rules are stable and well-understood (i.e., the first condition above). This fact exposes a basic dichotomy between the rules of measurement across the two different conditions, and it highlights the need to account for these tensions in measuring and predicting value. That is, when the rules for value creation are still being discovered (i.e., as in the second condition above), value is often created through new processes, capabilities, and technologies. These outcomes may seem to have little value by themselves at first, but they have potentially enormous spillover benefits for future activities. It is often difficult to identify these activities, however, and to quantify the value of these spillover benefits.

This brings us to the understanding provided in the field of economics using the concepts of concavity and convexity. Concavity helps us identify strategies for one condition, convexity for the other. More specifically, a concave function looks like the one depicted in Figure 6.1.

A concave function is characterized by diminishing marginal returns. That is, as one invests more, one receives more total return but less at the margin. For example, suppose that an individual invests $100 (i.e., 100 units of input), and the investment generates $185 in return (i.e., 185 units of output). In the concave condition illustrated in Figure 6.1, if that person increases the investment to a total of $200, the payout would be only $210. Whereas the total return increases, this represents an incremental output of only $25 in return for the additional $100 investment, or a diminishing marginal return.

All of us are familiar with concave functions in our daily lives. For example, when a person is very hungry, any morsel of food is seen as highly desirable – even Brussels spouts or turnip greens. However, as one becomes less hungry, or as a person approaches the satisfaction of the hunger need,

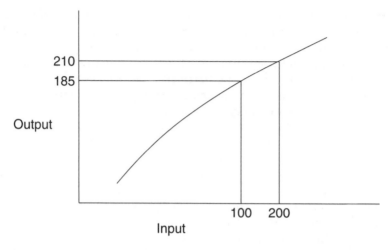

Figure 6.1 An example of a concave function

foods become marginally less attractive. This is typical of most physiological needs – the closer to satiation the less the motivation. A variety of
motivation theories are based on this presumption (i.e., need theories).

One product of concavity is risk aversion. That is, individuals usually
prefer expected or certain outcomes to risky outcomes, especially as the
stakes go up. For example, suppose that a 50 percent chance exists that a particular company will perform very well, and a 50 percent chance exists that
it will do poorly. Suppose also that the employees in this company are offered
the following two bonus options at the beginning of the year. (1) Employees
can receive a $100 000 bonus for the year regardless of the company's per-
formance. (2) Employees can receive a $200 000 bonus if the company does
very well but no bonus if the company does poorly. Both options have the
same expected value (i.e., $100 000 = 0.5 × $200 000 + 0.5 × 0), but it is
obvious that the second alternative has more risk associated with it. Many
individuals will tend to select the first option. That is, the risk aversion tendency of many people (assuming that they cannot directly control the performance of the firm) will lead them to prefer the sure pay out. In fact, if
they are sufficiently risk averse, employees may continue to prefer the first
option even if the amount associated with the second option is raised, say,
to $220 000. It may require a larger payoff than $220 000 to overcome the
tendency to take the safe bet.

When the rules of value creation are well known, concavity tends to dominate. When individuals know the rules – that is, they know the expected pay
out – they tend to avoid risking a sure thing for an unsure thing. Diminishing

marginal returns leads them to believe that investing beyond a certain point is not worthwhile. In the example above, even if employees selected the second option, the bonus would still be the same even if the company doubled or quadrupled its revenues. That is, beyond a certain point, the higher the organization performs, the smaller the incremental payoff.

Risk aversion, then, means minimizing levels of uncertainty, or opting for certainty over uncertainty. Limiting investments, limiting risk (e.g., shortening the time horizon over which value creation is judged), and proceeding incrementally are examples of ways people cope with conditions of concavity. In the case of the bonus system above, for example, it may be better to offer employees a base bonus of $50 000 regardless of how the company performs, plus an additional bonus of, say, $120 000 to be paid only if the company does especially well. The expected value of this additional $110 000 ($50 000 + 0.5 × $120 000 + 0.5 × 0) is the same as the offer of a $220 000 bonus, but it is far more likely to be selected. The risk has been substantially reduced because employees are not betting their entire bonus package on the company's success. This strategy is typical of firms who assiduously avoid 'betting the farm' on new products, new technologies, new markets, or other investments defined as risky. Concavity reduces the inclination toward risk.

Convexity, on the other hand, represents the exact opposite condition. Figure 6.2 shows the relationships between inputs and outputs.

A convex function is characterized by an increasing marginal return. That is, as an individual invests more, more total return is acquired as well

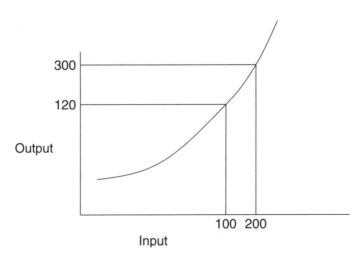

Figure 6.2   An example of a convex function

as incrementally more return at the margin. For example, suppose an individual invests $100 (i.e., 100 units of inputs) and receives a pay out of $120 (i.e., 120 units of output). The incremental output is $20 on the original investment. If, however, the same individual invests a total of $200 and receives $300 in return, the total output as well as the incremental output has increased. An additional $180 is received from an increase of $100 in investment, or a fourfold increase in the marginal return.

This convexity function is also typical of some motivation theories in the social sciences. For example, individual growth needs, needs for learning, or human virtues are needs that are not satisfied as need fulfillment is approached. In other words, the more one has an opportunity to grow, to learn, or to experience human virtues such as compassion and love, the more one is attracted to them and the higher the level of motivation. Investing more of oneself in those activities leads to an increasing motivation (the opposite of physiological needs) and an increasing marginal output. This is a condition of convexity.

One product of convexity is risk preference. That is, many individuals prefer the thrill of the gamble or the rush associated with the chance to win big compared to the more conservative stance of selecting a sure thing. Shooting fish in a barrel isn't much fun, they would say. Risk oriented people, for example, would much prefer bonus option number 2 (i.e., selecting the $200 000 option on the chance that company did well) at least partly because of the sense of risk involved. Gambling casinos and horse racing tracks are full of people with these kinds of preferences.

When the rules of value creation are still being discovered or are highly uncertain, convexity dominates. The promise of increasing marginal returns means that large investments are desirable. Even when marginal returns are uncertain, if the promise of potential payoffs is high, increasing investment is the preferred strategy. Investing in an entrepreneurial venture, fostering innovative initiatives, or engaging in transformational change all may be pursued because of the promise of a major pay out in the end.

EXAMPLES OF CONCAVITY AND CONVEXITY

Most large, mature organizations exist in a condition of concavity. For example, when the rules of engagement are well understood, when many firms are competing in the same market, and when the market size is well established and stable, a condition of concavity exists. When one firm increases the scale of its operations or improves market penetration, its gains must come at the expense of a competitor. Expansion of firm size or market share is usually achieved by reducing prices and accepting lower margins.

For example, Wal-Mart's annual return on net assets in 1987 was approximately 25 percent. That is, 25 cents was earned on every dollar invested by the firm. A strategy of massive growth was implemented shortly thereafter, and by 1992 a much larger Wal-Mart chain had an annual return of 17 percent. The total was larger but the margin was smaller.

In contrast, many small, entrepreneurial firms – or companies in rapidly developing or innovative industries – face a condition of convexity. The potential uses of technologies, products, or services are unknown or are being discovered. Firms compete in varied, often-unpredictable ways, and no accepted boundaries for the industry exist for a period of time. Thus, a firm may discover a new product, service, or application, and it will create its own rules of engagement. It invests rapidly in the new strategy, for example, to capitalize on first-entrant benefits. Marginal rates of return increase because competing firms are not yet able to compete head-to-head and to depress profit margins, and market size expands as new customers are found.

Examples of firms facing an environment of convexity include Amazon.com, AOL, and Microsoft, which have continually expanded the scope and market size of their firms. (Some may debate whether this has been done at the expense of or in spite of competitive firms.) Not only have total revenues expanded markedly, but margins have increased as new applications and new product lines have been created.

Concavity and convexity imply optimal rules that are diametrically opposed to one another. The desired outcomes and the strategies required to produce them are by and large opposite. Best practices for one tend to be worst practices for the other. For example, Table 6.1 illustrates this fundamental opposition.

In brief, conditions of concavity require precise measures and obvious payouts in the short-run. Conditions of convexity require long-term development and experimentation.

Of course, in the real world of organizations, leaders are often faced with the challenge of managing both kinds of conditions simultaneously. They must maintain core competencies and core businesses in core markets, while at the same time pursue innovative opportunities and ventures into heretofore-unknown territory. The technological and information revolutions have made these kinds of demands almost inevitable. Leaders must ensure immediate results while also investing in the future. They must be predictable and controlled as well as innovative and experimental. They must capture immediate return as well as ensure long-run return. They must be both risk-averse and risk-oriented.

Whereas the most capable leaders can manage such paradoxical tensions, the pursuit of diametrically opposed strategies simultaneously often creates

Table 6.1   Best and worst practices for concavity and convexity

Concavity best practice Convexity worst practice	Concavity worst practice Convexity best practice
Initiatives that produce the highest measurable financial rates of return in the near future are best.	Initiatives that create new technologies, processes, and brand equity are important even if they are achieved with low returns in the short run.
A firm's future value creation potential can be assessed on the basis of its past value creation performance.	A firm's past value creation performance is often meaningless in predicting future value creation.
Value can be measured quantitatively at all levels of the firm by converging upon a few key metrics.	Value is difficult to quantify because it is created through the development of new competencies and by conducting experiments in new territories.

tensions and friction in organizations. Instead of achieving success, leaders find themselves unable to satisfy either set of demands completely. That is where the Competing Values Framework becomes most useful. It assists leaders in managing long-run and short-run marginal returns.

COMPETING VALUES AND THE STOCK MARKET

For a publicly-traded company, the primary measure of whether the firm is effectively managing short-run and the long-run financial returns simultaneously is the firm's stock price. Investors reward firms that achieve both short-run profitability and long-run strength by increasing the amount of money they are willing to pay for a share of the firm's stock. The higher the stock price, the higher the firm's market value. Improving market value becomes, then, a primary objective of most leaders – that is, they seek to increase the price of the company's stock. The higher the firm's stock price the higher is the value the market attaches to the firm's future potential. Leaders become famous when they preside over dramatic increases in shareholder value. Witness the heroic aura that surrounded Jack Welch, under whose leadership GE's market value increased so dramatically, and Warren Buffet, who as CEO of Berkshire Hathaway, has been famous for consistently delivering high shareholder value.

Most measurement devices used to assess organizational performance do not account for the tensions inherent in managing for the short-run as well as the long-run, managing predictability as well as innovation, or managing for fast pay out as well as for future strength. The Competing Values Framework, on the other hand, has been used to identify criteria of performance in each of the four quadrants, and these very tensions are taken into account.

To address this issue, we have conducted extensive empirical research into the relationship of the Competing Values Framework with shareholder value. The findings of the research can be summarized as follows:

- There is a high statistical correlation between the variables of the Competing Values Framework and contemporaneous cross-sectional variations in market-value-to-book-value ratios of (publicly-traded) companies.
- The Competing Values Framework is also powerful in predicting *future* market values. Investing in a (value-weighted) portfolio of firms that are in the top quintile based on their competing values rankings consistently yields returns that are well above market returns as well as the returns required to compensate investors for the risk they bear from investing in these top-quintile portfolios.

Thus, it appears that the Competing Values Framework explains in a statistically significant way what the stock market considers of value in pricing companies. If one believes that the (U.S.) stock market is fairly efficient, then it must be true that the market looks beyond a firm's short-term financial performance and considers its capabilities to deliver future performance. The challenge is to figure out how it assesses these capabilities. While that is not the goal of the Competing Values Framework, it is interesting that the value-creation capabilities the Competing Values Framework emphasizes are also those that the market appears to consider important.

DESIGNING THE EMPIRICAL TESTS

There are two types of empirical tests that we have conducted: contemporaneous and predictive. Each is described below. In these tests, we assigned two variables (representing dimensions of value creation) to each of the four quadrants and then chose a proxy for each of these eight variables, as explained in Table 6.2.

A few words on these proxies are in order. Let us start with the Control quadrant. The two measures of value creation in this quadrant are quality and efficiency. Ideally, we would like to measure quality by directly assessing the quality of the firm's products and services. This is, however, not feasible given the number of firms in our database. So we made the assump-

Table 6.2   Two types of empirical tests

Quadrant	Measures for quadrant	Proxies used
Control	Quality	Gross margin
	Efficiency	Asset turnover
Compete	Profit	EVA
	Speed	Change in EVA growth
Create	Growth	Sales growth
	Innovation	Standard deviation of
		market model errors
Collaborate	Knowledge	Future growth values
	Community	Sales/number of employees

tion that the higher the firm's product quality, the higher will be the price premium it will be able to command and thus the higher will be its 'gross margin', defined as [sales revenue minus cost of goods sold] divided by sales revenue. As for efficiency, many measures are possible. The one we focus on is how efficiently the firm manages its asset base, since in recent years this efficiency measure has been the chief concern of investors and organizations alike. We thus use the classic definition of asset efficiency as our proxy, 'asset turnover', defined as sales, divided by assets in a given year.

Let us now move to the Compete quadrant, where the two measures of value creation are profit and speed. By profit, we mean 'economic profit' rather than accounting net income, which is subject to all sorts of manipulations and distortions, as the events in 2002 with WorldCom, Enron, Tyco, and others have aptly illustrated. The commonly-used notion of economic profits is Economic Valued Added (EVA), which is defined as Net Operating Profits After Tax (NOPAT), minus a capital charge, where capital charge equals the firm's weighted-average cost of capital, times Net Assets Deployed. By speed, we mean the speed with which initiatives are executed and hence economic profit is improved. We thus create a proxy for speed by the change in the firm's EVA growth rate from one year to the next, over a five-year time period.

Turning to the Create quadrant, the two measures of value creation are growth and innovation. We adopt a fairly conventional view of growth – it is the rate at which the company's sales are growing. Thus, the proxy for growth is sales growth. Innovation is something we would ideally like to assess by measuring the success of the company's innovation efforts in terms of its products, services, and business designs. This is difficult to do directly given data limitations. So, we took an indirect approach. As has been done in some recent finance research, we view a firm's 'idiosyncratic stock return risk' as a proxy for its innovativeness. The idea is as follows. A firm's stock returns are driven by two factors: its co-movement with the overall market (or economy) and its idiosyncratic circumstances. The more innovative the firm becomes, the more different it looks from the rest of the herd, namely, the overall market, and hence, the greater is the influence of its own idiosyncratic factors in driving its stock returns, relative to the influence of the overall market. We measure idiosyncratic stock return risk by measuring the standard deviation of the firm's idiosyncratic returns, i.e., the difference between its actual returns and the portion of the returns that can be explained by co-movement with the overall market return.

The final quadrant is Collaborate, where the measures of value creation are knowledge and community. Organization knowledge is a highly complex variable and difficult to measure directly. So we focus on knowledge that leads to perceptions of future value creation, since the unique knowledge the organization possesses today, to the extent that it has value relevance, should lead to value creation in the future. Thus, our proxy for knowledge is 'future growth value', which is defined as the differences between the firm's current market value (which impounds investors' expectations of future value creation) and what its market value would be if its profits (NOPAT) did not grow. That is, it is the portion of the firm's current market capitalization that is attributable to expectations about future growth, which, in turn, is ostensibly driven by the unique knowledge assets the firm possesses. As for community, what we really want to measure is one of the softest aspects of the organization – the quality of its internal community. We have the instruments with which we can do this if we were to go inside an organization and interview employees. This, however, is precluded from a database as large as the one used in our analysis. So we made the assumption that the greater the impact an individual employee has on the success of the organization, the more 'relevant' that employee will feel, and the greater will be the sense of 'ownership' and internal community. Thus, we created a proxy for community with a variable defined as sales/number of employees. The more the organization sells per employee, the greater the sense of community.

These proxies are not perfect, of course, but they serve as approximations of objective financial measures in each of the quadrants. Inasmuch as publicly available financial data were used for data on these companies, we determined that these proxies were as representative of each quadrant as any others that might be selected.

CONTEMPORANEOUS ANALYSIS

This battery of tests involves explaining cross-sectional variations in market-value-to-book-value ratios with the help of competing values variables from the four quadrants, using the eight proxies explained above.

We use the ordinary least squares (OLS) multivariate regression technique in which the dependent variable is the ratio of market value of total assets to book value of total assets for each firm in the sample in a given year, for the various dimensions of the primary competencies of the Competing Values Framework for the *same* year. Market value is defined as market value of equity plus book value of debt, where market value of equity is the common stock price per share times the number of shares outstanding.

We conduct this analysis for a sample of 2300–3000 publicly traded firms for each year from 1991 through 1999. The results are reported below. Note that the number associated with multiple R informs us about the statistical correlation (minimum −1 to maximum +1) between cross-sectional variations in market-value-to-book-value ratios and the proxies for the competing values variables. The 'F value' indicates the statistical significance of the regression (the higher the F value the better). The 'confidence level' of the significance is based directly on the F value (the higher the confidence level, the smaller is the likelihood that the documented results are due to pure chance). *NS* refers to nonsignificant relationships.

The analysis is conducted for the entire sample as well as for six industries derived from the SIC codes in the Compustat database; traditional manufacturing, manufacturing-chemical processes, manufacturing machinery and high-tech equipment, wholesale trade, retail trade, and services (see Table 6.3).

These results indicate that the measures of the Competing Values Framework do a good job of explaining cross-sectional variations in market-to-book-value ratios.

PREDICTIVE ANALYSIS

For the predictive analysis, we examined the ability of the competing values variables in a given year to predict cross-sectional variations in market-value-to-book-value ratios the *following* year. The results are reported in Table 6.4. Note that the results for 1994, for example, use competing values variables for 1994 and market-value-to-book-value ratios for 1995, so that we were interested in determining the extent to which financial performance could be predicted in advance.

Table 6.3 Explaining variations in value, 1991–99

Statistics	Entire sample	Traditional manufacturing	Manufacturing-chemical processes	Manufacturing-machinery and hi-tech equipment	Wholesale trade	Retail trade	Services
1991							
Multiple R	0.2	0.56	0.36	0.3	0.73	0.25	0.22
F-Value	13.8	14.65	5.95	9.37	16.55	1.38	1.488
Regression statistically significant at confidence level of	99%	99%	99%	99%	99%	NS	NS
Number of observations	2645	262	313	759	121	164	231
1992							
Multiple R	0.21	0.61	0.34	0.33	0.56	0.26	0.22
F-Value	16.43	19.51	5.37	12.39	7.86	1.61	1.55
Regression statistically significant at confidence level of	99%	99%	99%	99%	99%	NS	NS
Number of observations	2804	270	334	786	140	180	251

Year								
1993	Multiple R	0.26	0.53	0.47	0.24	0.48	0.58	0.43
	F-Value	26.67	12.98	12.27	6.2	4.8	11.1	7.11
	Regression statistically significant at confidence level of	99%	99%	99%	99%	99%	99%	99%
	Number of observations	2828	275	342	794	136	183	253
1994	Multiple R	0.17	0.54	0.51	0.29	0.69	0.48	0.17
	F-Value	10.99	14.03	15.42	9.17	15.11	6.62	0.97
	Regression statistically significant at confidence level of	99%	99%	99%	99%	NS		
	Number of observations	2811	271	350	798	137	183	253
1995	Multiple R	0.25	0.63	0.43	0.24	0.49	0.21	0.39
	F-Value	24.7	22.39	10.23	6.38	5.19	1.08	5.59
	Regression statistically significant at confidence level of	99%	99%	99%	99%	99%	NS	99%
	Number of observations	2827	279	354	807	136	186	255

Table 6.3 (continued)

Statistics	Entire sample	Traditional manufacturing	Manufacturing-chemical processes	Manufacturing-machinery and hi-tech equipment	Wholesale trade	Retail trade	Services
1996							
Multiple R	0.31	0.67	0.45	0.28	0.56	0.24	0.38
F-Value	39.53	27.72	11.9	8.9	6.9	1.51	5.62
Regression statistically significant at confidence level of	99%	99%	99%	99%	99%	NS	99%
Number of observations	2898	280	388	804	130	204	266
1997							
Multiple R	0.29	0.68	0.51	0.33	0.45	0.35	0.54
F-Value	34.45	29.96	16.31	12.37	3.83	3.77	13.94
Regression statistically significant at confidence level of	99%	99%	99%	99%	95%	95%	99%
Number of observations	2918	267	379	812	127	219	274

1998	Multiple R	0.2	0.63	0.27	0.28	0.78	0.35	0.31
	F-Value	16.51	23.4	3.86	8.65	23.54	3.98	3.84
	Regression statistically significant at confidence level of	99%	99%	95%	99%	99%	95%	95%
	Number of observations	3008	292	389	811	130	226	289
1999	Multiple R	0.21	0.54	0.39	0.27	0.54	0.6	0.18
	F-Value	17.17	13.04	8.02	7.74	5.92	14.4	1.21
	Regression statistically significant at confidence level of	99%	99%	99%	99%	99%	99%	NS
	Number of observations	2811	254	351	745	125	206	273

Table 6.4 Predicting future changes in value, 1991–99

	Statistics	Entire sample	Traditional manufacturing	Manufacturing-chemical processes	Manufacturing-machinery and hi-tech equipment	Wholesale trade	Retail trade	Services
1991	Multiple R	0.18	0.58	0.52	0.26	0.74	0.3	0.22
	F-Value	20.8	15.4	8.97	11.54	3.27	2.04	2.58
	Regression statistically significant at confidence level of	99%	99%	99%	99%	99%	NS	NS
	Number of observations	2645	262	313	759	121	164	231
1992	Multiple R	0.23	0.56	0.42	0.32	0.4	0.29	0.28
	F-Value	20.8	15.4	8.97	11.54	3.27	2.04	2.58
	Regression statistically significant at confidence level of	99%	99%	99%	99%	99%	NS	NS
	Number of observations	2804	270	334	786	140	180	251

Year		C1	C2	C3	C4	C5	C6	C7
1993	Multiple R	0.42	0.51	0.57	0.26	0.74	0.53	0.67
	F-Value	77.18	12.24	20.19	7.5	20.12	8.83	24.88
	Regression statistically significant at confidence level of	99%	99%	99%	99%	99%	99%	99%
	Number of observations	2828	275	342	794	136	183	253
1994	Multiple R	0.21	0.42	0.47	0.27	0.46	0.4	0.28
	F-Value	16.8	6.99	12.5	8.18	4.33	4.34	2.6
	Regression statistically significant at confidence level of	99%	99%	99%	99%	95%	95%	NS
	Number of observations	2811	271	350	798	137	183	253
1995	Multiple R	0.3	0.63	0.45	0.24	0.5	0.27	0.4
	F-Value	34.57	22.67	10.99	5.97	5.5	1.8	5.85
	Regression statistically significant at confidence level of	99%	99%	99%	99%	95%	NS	99%
	Number of observations	2827	279	354	807	136	186	255

Table 6.4 (continued)

Statistics	Entire sample	Traditional manufacturing	Manufacturing-chemical processes	Manufacturing-machinery and hi-tech equipment	Wholesale trade	Retail trade	Services
1996							
Multiple R	0.35	0.66	0.58	0.225	0.53	0.3	0.25
F-Value	50.76	25.87	21.68	5.312	5.93	2.47	2.199
Regression statistically significant at confidence level of	99%	99%	99%	95%	99%	NS	NS
Number of observations	2898	280	388	804	130	204	266
1997							
Multiple R	0.24	0.36	0.31	0.35	0.41	0.41	0.3
F-Value	23.17	5.16	4.96	14.47	2.99	5.38	5.6
Regression statistically significant at confidence level of	95%	95%	95%	99%	NS	95%	95%
Number of observations	2918	287	379	812	127	219	274

1998	Multiple R	0.19	0.56	0.33	0.23	0.44	0.57	0.2
	F-Value	13.96	16.64	5.89	5.81	3.82	13.3	1.6
	Regression statistically significant at confidence level of	99%	99%	99%	99%	95%	99%	NS
	Number of observations	3006	292	389	811	130	228	289
1999	Multiple R	0.25	0.4	0.41	0.5	0.42	0.33	0.24
	F-Value	25.12	5.9	9.11	31.04	3.24	3.16	2.08
	Regression statistically significant at confidence level of	95%	99%	99%	99%	95%	90%	NS
	Number of observations	2611	254	351	745	125	206	273

Table 6.5   *Competing values top 20 percent portfolio and its relative*
                 performance

Holding period	Realized return on competing values top quintile (%)	Time synchronized market return (%)	Expected return on competing values top quintile based on risk (%)	Abnormal return on competing values top quintile (%)
2000	14	−8	11	3
1999	14	24	13	1
1998	27	21	13	14
1997	36	31	13	23
1996	28	21	15	13
1995	39	34	14	25
1994	4	1	15	−11
1993	16	11	15	1

From Table 6.5 we see that the Competing Values Framework predicts much of the cross-sectional variations in future ratios of market value to book value. More important, the tests produce results that are statistically significant. To further test the ability of the framework to enable one to predict the dynamics of stock market valuation, we conducted another test. We constructed portfolios based on how firms were ranked based on the competing values measures, and we assigned each firm a percentile score based on where that firm ranked relative to all the other firms in the sample. Then, we added up the scores for that firm across all the competing values proxies to come up with a single score for each firm. This represented the firm's competing values score. For a given year, say year t, we constructed a portfolio consisting of the top quintile of competing values firms, i.e. the top 20 percent based on the competing values scores. After this we computed the return one would have earned by holding this portfolio from year t to t+1. Note that the expected return on the competing values top quintile portfolio is computed using the Capital Asset Pricing Model (CAPM). This is done by computing the portfolio (a measure of systematic risk) and then computing the expected return as the risk free rate (long-term Treasury bond rate) plus the beta (β) times a 7 percent market risk premium. More plainly, the abnormal return is the realized return minus the expected return.

From these tests, it appears that not only is the Competing Values Framework useful in understanding how the stock market values

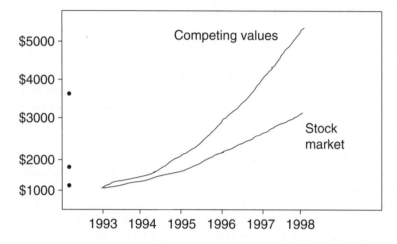

Figure 6.3   *Stock market performance versus competing values performance*

companies, but is also incisive in its description of stock price *dynamics* since it is efficient in predicting future movements of stock prices. In all but one year (1999), the competing values top-quintile portfolio beat the market, and in all but one year (1994) the competing values top-quintile portfolio earns an abnormally high return given its risk.

To illustrate the dramatic difference this excess in financial return produces over time, another comparison was made between the two portfolios – competing values top-quartile versus the average stock market portfolio. Suppose that investors were to invest $1000 in the two portfolios in 1993, and then subsequently reinvest the interest gained every year until 1998. Figure 6.3 shows that the competing values top quartile portfolio would be worth almost $5000 whereas the average stock portfolio would have increased to approximately $3000.

It is clear that the Competing Values Framework enhances understanding of how the stock market evaluates and values companies. Yet, it is even more useful in being able to predict *future* market value. The framework does so by capturing in financial measures the simultaneous opposites faced by leaders and organizations in the modern world. Internal and external demands, maintaining stability and flexibility, moving fast and moving slow all are captured in the Competing Values Framework. These financial measures, it can be seen, assess firm performance in a way that exceeds normal financial analysis.

COMPETING VALUES PROFILES

One final way in which we analysed company performance was to compare individual companies with their own industry's averages on each of the competing values financial measures. Since firms that did well on the competing values measures exceeded normal organizations' performance, we were interested in addressing the question: What is the impact of having a company exceed the industry average on any particular financial measure? Can individual firms enhance their financial revenues by improving their scores on specific competing values measures?

In Figures 6.4 and 6.5, the scores of the giant retailer, Sears, and of the technology firm, Hewlett-Packard, are represented on each of the competing values measures. An industry average score is also represented on the same chart – the retail trade industry in the case of Sears, and the computer services industry in the case of Hewlett-Packard. (The plots in these figures are computed on the basis of standardized scores, but the scales have been omitted to reduce clutter. The key differences being illustrated are evident without the scales being reproduced.) Note that in the case of Sears, performance exceeds the industry average on the Innovation and Quality mea-

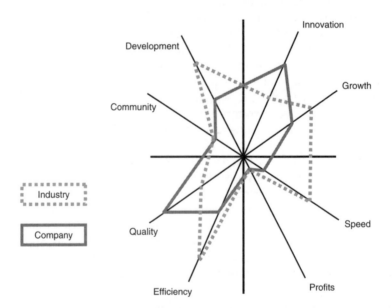

Figure 6.4   Sears performance on competing values dimensions relative to industry average for the year 2000

sures and trails the industry average on Development, Community, Efficiency, Profits, Speed and Growth. Similarly, Hewlett-Packard outperforms the industry average on the Community, Efficiency, and Speed measures and underperforms relative to the industry average on Development, Quality, Profits, Growth, and Innovation.

The figures show that Sears underperforms relative to the industry average on, for example, the efficiency measure by a large margin. Similarly, Hewlett-Packard underperforms relative to the industry average by a large margin on the innovation measure.

Financial analyses demonstrate that if Sears were to increase its performance on the efficiency dimension by just one standard deviation relative to the industry, the payoff in market value would total $7.88 billion dollars per year. If Hewlett-Packard were to increase its performance on the innovation dimension by just one standard deviation relative to the industry, the payoff in market value would total $12.78 billion.

Of course, an emphasis in one area requires a de-emphasis in another since resources (including time, money, and human commitment) are limited, so both firms would be unwise to abandon all other activities to pursue improvement on a single financial measurement. Trade-offs are always inevitable. What is important, however, is that the Competing

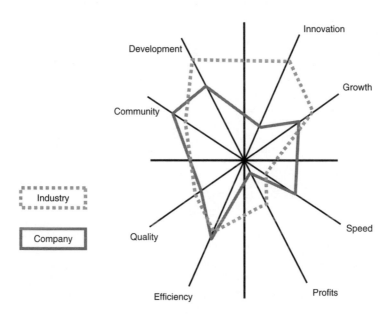

Figure 6.5   Hewlett-Packard performance on competing values dimensions relative to industry average for the year 2000

Values Framework can serve as a powerful tool in helping leaders better understand and measure the financial performance of their organizations.

The Competing Values Framework excels, in other words, at providing guidance to leaders for managing concavity and convexity, making relative trade-offs on competing criteria, and offering benchmarks against which to compare firm performance. It predicts both current and future market performance, and it can provide organizations with prescriptions regarding the areas in which investment of time and resources should be made. Because the framework measures both performance and capability, it represents a new approach to assessing value creation as well as providing a blueprint for creating future value.

7. Measuring leadership competencies and organizational culture

In the previous chapter we described the measures used to assess financial performance in companies based on the Competing Values Framework. We demonstrated how the Competing Values Framework provides indicators of financial performance that accurately predict both current and future market value of firms. Companies do better financially if they utilize the full spectrum of measures advocated by the Competing Values Framework. In this chapter we shift to measurements of leadership competencies, and organizational culture. We also provide examples of other assessment tools associated with the Competing Values Framework, namely, Organizational Outcomes and Organizational Change Strategies.

The Competing Values Framework provides a way for leaders to assess their own competencies, their organization's culture, and, based on those measurements, to develop a personal development plan and improvement agenda. The extent to which leaders have developed certain key competencies, and the extent to which personal competencies match the organization's culture, serve as standards that guide development plans and improvement agendas.

LEADERSHIP EFFECTIVENESS

Never has there been a time when effective leadership is more crucial for organizational success. This is because of the dramatic increase in the challenges experienced by virtually every organizational sector – large and small, public and private, old-economy and new-economy. Each is faced with hyper-turbulent speed, information revolution, dramatic increases in technological innovation, and unpredictable global events. No one doubts that the next decade will be characterized by chaotic, transformational, rapid-fire change. In fact, almost no sane person is willing to predict what the world will be like 25, 10, or even 5 years from now. Change is just too rapid and ubiquitous. The development of 'nanobombs' have caused some people to predict that personal computers and desk top monitors will land on the scrap heap of obsolescence within 15 years. The new computers will be a product of etchings on molecules leading to personalized data processors injected into the bloodstream, implanted in eyeglasses, or included in wristwatches.

Despite all this change in our environment, something has remained, and continues to remain, relatively constant. With minor variations and stylistic differences, what has not changed, in several thousand years, are the basic skills that lie at the heart of effective, satisfying, growth-producing human relationships. Freedom, dignity, trust, and honesty in relationships have always been among the goals of human beings, and the same principles that brought about those outcomes in the eleventh century still bring them about in the twenty-first century. Despite our circumstances, in other words, and despite the technological resources we have available to us, the same basic human skills still lie at the heart of effective human interaction. Human relationships are becoming more important, not less, as the information age unfolds and technologies encroach even more on our daily lives. Whereas the 'technological float' (the time it takes to develop a technology from the time it is introduced) has plummeted dramatically in recent years, the 'human float' (the time it takes to build an effective, developmental relationship) remains almost the same as always.

Extensive research by management scholars has identified critical competencies that characterize the most effective leaders and the most effective organizations worldwide. It is not unusual, however, for firms to generate a list of competencies for their own managers and leaders but to over-emphasize or under-emphasize one of the quadrants in the Competing Values Framework. For example, before beginning to work with the Competing Values Framework, Dana Corporation had articulated a list of key managerial competencies that over-emphasized Control and Compete quadrants and under-emphasized Create quadrant competencies. Several of the business units in Philips Electronics (e.g., Medical Systems, Passive Components, Domestic Appliances) had created competency lists that also were out of balance, over-emphasizing one or two quadrants and ignoring another. A list of competencies created for Philips by an external consulting firm, for example, ended up orienting almost all highly valued competencies to the Create quadrant. It took the imposition of the Competing Values Framework to help diagnose the extent to which their desired leadership competencies represented not a set of well-rounded skills required for effective performance but a narrow set of competencies focused on temporary challenges. In this chapter, we introduce an instrument that assesses 20 key areas of leadership competency that are based on the Competing Values Framework.

The leadership skills being assessed were not arbitrarily selected. They were derived from more than a dozen studies of leadership effectiveness conducted by the authors and by others. These competencies have been found to be predictive of personal and organizational effectiveness (Cameron, 2005c). In one study of managers on three continents, for example, 74 percent of successful managers had demonstrated high competency in these skills, whereas this was the case in only 24 percent of the failures. A study at PepsiCo found that company units headed by managers with well-developed people skills (including those assessed here) outperformed yearly revenue targets by 15 to 20 percent. Those with under-developed skills under-performed their targets by about the same amount. A study of University of California at Berkeley PhDs over 40 years found that people skills were four times more powerful than IQ in predicting who achieved success in their field – even for hard scientists. A McBer (consulting firm) study comparing outstanding managers with average managers found that 90 percent of the difference was accounted for by competency in the managerial skills assessed here. In a worldwide study of what companies were looking for in hiring new employees, 67 percent of the most desired attributes were these competencies. In a study of highly competent partners in a consulting firm, in which they were compared to partners with average people management skills, 41 percent of the high 'people management' group had been promoted after two years whereas only 10 percent of the low 'people management' partners had been promoted. More importantly, the highly competent 'people management' partners contributed more than twice as much revenue to the company as did the less competent partners.

The point of these studies, of course, is that effective leaders have developed high levels of competency in the areas assessed by the Leadership Competencies Survey introduced in this chapter.

THE LEADERSHIP COMPETENCIES SURVEY

Research including more than 80 000 managers and executives has resulted in several core conclusions regarding this instrument. Among the most important are:

1. The most effective managers have at least average competency on leadership skills in all four quadrants. They do not have blind spots and major areas of weakness in any of the quadrants. This does not mean that they are excellent in all four quadrants. They may lack certain strengths or have areas in which they are less competent. Effective leaders, however, possess the ability to perform at adequate levels or better in all four quadrants.
2. The most effective leaders have highly developed skills in the quadrants that are congruent with their organization's dominant culture. That is,

most organizations adopt a certain dominant culture over time. That cultural dominance can be assessed and described by instruments based on the Competing Values Framework (see Cameron and Quinn, 2006). Demonstrating leadership competencies in the quadrants that dominate the organization's culture is associated with higher levels of success for the leader.

3. Both underdeveloped skill levels as well as an overemphasis on particular skills inhibit leadership effectiveness. We have described several times the 'negative zones' that occur if an individual gives too much emphasis to one quadrant. Too much focus on control, for example, leads to frozen bureaucracy. Our research confirms our claims in Chapter 3 that paradoxical and flexible leadership is the most effective leadership (e.g., being able to be both soft and hard or both fast and slow simultaneously). Being extraordinarily competent interpersonally, for example, without competency in other quadrants does not produce effective leadership.

4. Leadership competency in each quadrant has a positive association with organizational performance. In Table 7.1, for example, the correlations between leadership competency and two measures of organizational performance are reported for a sample of approximately 57 000 managers.

The numbers in the cells are the correlations between leader scores on competencies in each quadrant and two measures of organizational performance: (1) the extent to which the organization improved over last year's

Table 7.1   Relationships between leadership competency and organizational performance

Quadrant	Performance over the last year	Performance relative to the competition	Manager's own salary increase
Collaborate competencies	0.324 $p < 0.000$	0.288 $p < 0.000$	0.084
Create competencies	0.351 $p < 0.000$	0.340 $p < 0.000$	0.095
Compete competencies	0.330 $p < 0.000$	0.367 $p < 0.000$	0.108
Control competencies	0.310 $p < 0.000$	0.322 $p < 0.000$	0.076

Note: 'p' indicates the probability that this result occurred by chance.

performance, and (2) the extent to which the organization performed better than its competitors. In each case, the probability is much less than 1 in 1000, indicating that one can be confident that the relationships are not a happenstance occurrence.

By way of contrast, we have also reported in Table 7.1 the relationship between personal leadership competency and personal salary increases. The low correlations indicate that scoring high on leadership competencies does not necessarily lead to the receipt of a higher than normal salary increase. The payoff of enhanced leadership competency, in other words, is more likely to be organizational improvement than personal reward.

Table 7.2 lists the 20 competencies assessed in the Leadership Competencies Survey. The complete instrument assesses these 20 leadership competencies, identifies the importance of each competency in an individual's own organization, assesses the extent to which the leader integrates or trades-off competing competencies, measures the organization's culture, and evaluates the leader's overall performance. The instrument itself consists of three items for each competency as well as assessments of various indicators of performance. The importance of each competency area for each leader's role is also assessed.

The instrument assesses competencies, not style, personality, temperament, or attitudes. Its aim is to illuminate the ways in which leaders actually behave at work, and thus assist them to capitalize on their strengths and work to build up under-developed areas. The instrument is available from the authors along with the opportunity to receive feedback reports comparing individual scores on the 20 competencies to scores in a data set of approximately 80 000 managers and 5000 organizations.

We generally use the Leadership Competencies Survey as a 360-degree feedback instrument in which individual leaders receive ratings from subordinates, peers, and superiors. That way, individual leaders can compare their own self-ratings with the perceptions of others with whom they work. When the instrument is administered in this way, we encourage leaders to use the feedback as a developmental tool. That is, the data are best used to help formulate a personal improvement agenda and/or a development strategy for the long-term. The instrument is not useful if it leads either to a sense of self-satisfaction and complacency or a sense of discouragement and desperation because of extremely high or low ratings. Almost all individuals in our experience receive significant benefit from receiving feedback using this instrument.

In general, feedback received from the instrument consists of:

1.   Average self-ratings on the 20 competencies;
2.   Average associates' ratings on the 20 competencies;

Table 7.2   Competencies assessed in the leadership competencies survey

Quadrant	Competency	Brief description
Collaborate quadrant competencies	Leading through teamwork	Building effective, cohesive, smooth functioning teams
	Leading through interpersonal relationships	Building effective relationships through communication and listening
	Leading the development of human capital	Helping others improve performance and develop competency
	Leading through cooperation and community	Fostering a sense of unity through involvement and empowerment
	Leading through compassion and caring	Facilitating a climate of personal concern and support for others
Create quadrant competencies	Leading through innovation and entrepreneurship	Encouraging others to innovate and to generate new ideas
	Leading the future	Communicating a clear vision and facilitating its accomplishment
	Leading through improvement and change	Fostering an inclination toward improvement and bold initiatives
	Leading through creativity	Helping to generate creativity both in oneself and in others
	Leading through flexibility and agility	Facilitating nimbleness and an ability to quickly adjust in the face of constant change
Compete quadrant competencies	Leading through competitiveness	Fostering an orientation toward beating the competition and winning in the marketplace
	Leading through customer relationships	Fostering a focus on relationships with and service of customers
	Leading through speed	Driving for faster responses and timelier actions
	Leading with intensity	Creating a focus on intense, hard work and achievement

Table 7.2   (continued)

Quadrant	Competency	Brief description
	Leading for results	Emphasizing even higher levels of performance and exceeding the competition
Control quadrant competencies	Leading through rational analysis	Fostering systematic analysis of problems, and relying on data for solving problems
	Leading through information clarity	Helping others to be clear about expectations, goals, and policies and their place in the enterprise
	Leading through high reliability	Eliminating mistakes and ensuring accuracy and precision in work
	Leading through processes	Ensuring smooth flowing processes and consistency of outputs
	Leading through measurement	Measuring and keeping records of how the organization is performing

3.   Self-ratings on the 60 individual items on the survey;
4.   Associates' ratings on the 60 individual items on the survey;
5.   A range of ratings received from associates, including the highest and lowest scores;
6.   A percentile rank for each of the 20 competencies and for the 60 items, based on a comparison with 80 000 other managers;
7.   Subordinates ratings of all competencies and items, as well as the range of ratings received;
8.   Peer ratings of all competencies and items, as well as the range of ratings received;
9.   Superior ratings of all competencies and items, as well as the range of ratings received;
10.   Ratings of the importance of the various competencies and items being assessed to achieving success in the leader's own job;
11.   Evaluations by associates of the effectiveness of the leader.

In using the instrument for development purposes, we always provide individuals with comparisons using the overall database. They receive a percentile ranking on each leadership competency showing how they score relative to approximately 80 000 other managers from all five continents – sometimes tailored for their own industry or functional area. Approximately 5000 organizations in multiple industries and sectors – including private, public, and not-for-profit organizations – are represented in the database. Individuals also receive comparisons between their own self ratings and the ratings of their subordinates, peers, and superiors. Obtaining a sense of the congruence between the leader's own self-perceptions and the perceptions of others, plus the congruence of perceptions among the subordinates, peers, and superiors themselves, is usually a very enlightening and useful set of data. These results help identify leadership strengths that can be built upon, the areas that leaders may want to improve, and the areas in which relationships with associates may need attention.

One example of an overall profile received by an individual using the instrument is shown in Figure 7.1. It shows the self-ratings of one randomly selected leader along with a combined rating of her subordinates, peers, and superiors. Using just this diagram alone, it is possible to identify areas of strength, areas potentially needing development, and areas where discrepancies between self-perceptions and colleagues' perceptions are greatest. In this figure, the leader rates herself significantly higher in all quadrants than her associates, with the largest discrepancies being in the Collaborate and Create quadrants. Associates' scores are much lower in those two quadrants, relatively speaking, than in the Compete and Control quadrants. The leader has a relatively well-rounded self-rating, but the associates' data shows higher ratings in the bottom two quadrants and relatively low ratings in the upper two quadrants.

This profile, of course, shows just one of the multiple types of data provided by the instrument, but it does bring to mind questions that a leader would want to address when using this feedback:

1. On which specific competencies are the discrepancies greatest between your own ratings and those of your associates (and among your associates)?
2. To what extent is your competency profile strong in all four quadrants (balanced), and to what extent are the ratings of your associates strong in all four quadrants?
3. Based on these results, in which competency areas are you especially strong?
4. In what areas does the most improvement seem to be indicated?
5. What specific behaviors can be implemented that will positively affect your own competencies – either capitalizing on strengths or building up underdeveloped areas?

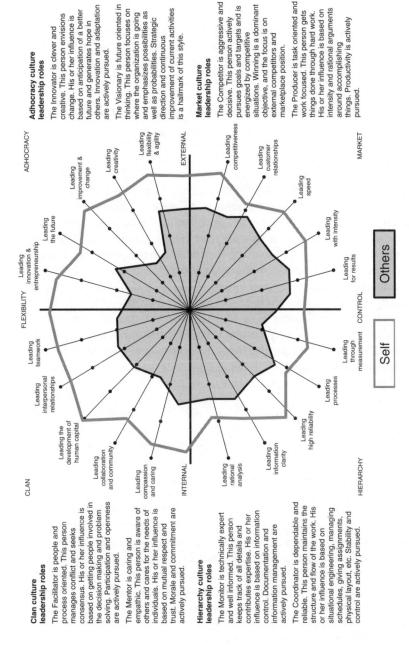

Clan culture leadership roles

The Facilitator is people and process oriented. This person manages conflict and seeks consensus. His or her influence is based on getting people involved in the decision making and problem solving. Participation and openness are actively pursued.

The Mentor is caring and empathic. This person is aware of others and cares for the needs of individuals. His or her influence is based on mutual respect and trust. Morale and commitment are actively pursued.

Hierarchy culture leadership roles

The Monitor is technically expert and well informed. This person keeps track of all details and contributes expertise. His or her influence is based on information control. Documentation and information management are actively pursued.

The Coordinator is dependable and reliable. This person maintains the structure and flow of the work. His or her influence is based on situational engineering, managing schedules, giving assignments, physical layout, etc. Stability and control are actively pursued.

Adhocracy culture leadership roles

The Innovator is clever and creative. This person envisions change. His or her influence is based on anticipation of a better future and generates hope in others. Innovation and adaptation are actively pursued.

The Visionary is future oriented in thinking. This person focuses on where the organization is going and emphasizes possibilities as well as probabilities. Strategic direction and continuous improvement of current activities is a hallmark of this style.

Market culture leadership roles

The Competitor is aggressive and decisive. This person actively pursues goals and targets and is energized by competitive situations. Winning is a dominant objective, and the focus is on external competitors and marketplace position.

The Producer is task oriented and work focused. This person gets things done through hard work. His or her influence is based on intensity and rational arguments around accomplishing things. Productivity is actively pursued.

Self   Others

Figure 7.1   An example of one leader's competency profile

6. Specifically, when will you begin, who else will be involved, how will you measure results, how will you maintain accountability?

These kinds of questions are simply meant to assist leaders formulate a useful improvement agenda or action plan – with appropriate social support, benchmarks, measurements, timelines, and accountability.

ASSESSING ORGANIZATIONAL CULTURE

In addition to comparisons with associates' perceptions, leaders also need to understand the nature of the organization in which they are operating. Leading an R&D lab may require different kinds of competencies than leading a manufacturing facility, for example. Leading a small entrepreneurial software firm may demand a different leadership profile than leading a 100-year-old transportation company. These potential organizational differences point out why we have also included in the Leadership Competencies Survey a measuring instrument that assesses the organization's culture. It identifies the culture of the organization in which the leader is managing (see Cameron and Quinn, 2006, for a complete discussion of The Organizational Culture Assessment Instrument).

As discussed in Chapter 3, as organizations progress through their life cycles, they tend to develop certain dominant cultural attributes. Culture refers to the core values, assumptions, definitions, and memories embedded in an organization. Much of the time, culture is ignored because it is taken for granted. Few of us woke up this morning and made a conscious decision about which language we would speak today. Our language is cultural and, hence, taken for granted. Like atomic particles that are measured by the effects they create rather than by the particles themselves, so culture can be assessed by observing its manifestations. Cultural attributes are reflected by processes such as the managerial style, strategic direction, climate, reward system, means of bonding people together, and vision that exist in the organization. When identifying the competencies on which leaders want to improve, it is crucial to understand the dominant cultural characteristics in their organization so that their development can occur in congruence with that culture. As mentioned before, research suggests that leaders are most effective when they possess competencies that match the organization's dominant culture. We include the Organizational Culture Assessment Instrument (OCAI) in the assessment package in order to identify the cultural profile of the leader's own organization.

In Figure 7.2, we illustrate the cultural profiles of six randomly selected firms in different sectors or industries. Each of these organizations is highly

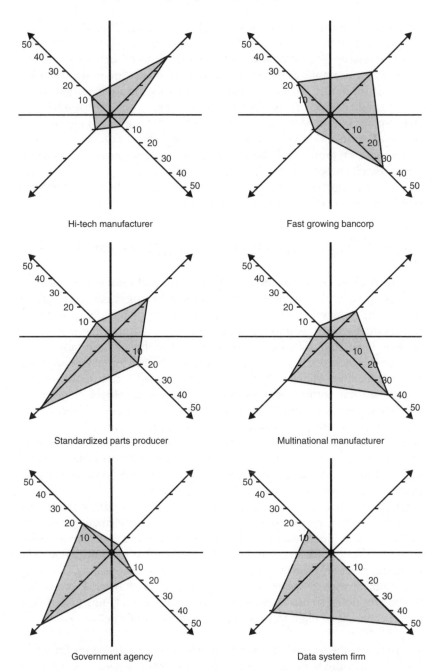

Hi-tech manufacturer

Fast growing bancorp

Standardized parts producer

Multinational manufacturer

Government agency

Data system firm

Figure 7.2 An example of six organizational cultural profiles

successful in its own industry or sector. The usefulness of analysing such a culture profile is that leaders' improvement plans and development strategies can be guided by the core values and dominant culture of their organizations.

Look, for example, at the government agency's culture in the lower left corner of the figure. To be most effective in this organization, leaders would want to make certain that they developed competency in Control skills since that type of culture dominates in this government agency. This does not mean, of course, that other skills are not important, nor that the leader cannot be even more highly developed in other competency areas. Rather, our research shows that for leaders to be effective, they must have well-developed competencies in the skills represented by their organization's dominant culture (Cameron and Quinn, 2006).

USES OF ORGANIZATIONAL CULTURE PROFILES

One of the ways in which the OCAI has been used most often and most effectively is in the diagnosis and changing of organizational culture. That is, the Competing Values Framework makes possible the opportunity for leaders to diagnose and implement an actual culture change initiative in their organizations. In order to achieve their highest aspirations and accomplish their goals, many leaders know that their organizations must undergo a culture change. They need to shift toward a more Collaborative culture so that commitment, empowerment, and employee engagement typify the firm. Or, they must shift toward a Compete culture so that customer relationships, competitiveness, and speed are characteristic of all activities in the company. Regardless of the culture change this is desired, up to now few if any valid and reliable processes were available to facilitate that task in a systematic way. The application of the Competing Values Framework now makes it a straitforward process.

One of the difficulties in organizations faced with the desire to implement culture change is that no language had existed, no key elements or dimensions had been identified, and no common perspective had been available to know what to talk about and on what elements to focus attention. The Competing Values Framework provides an intuitively appealing and easily interpretable way to foster the process of culture change. A prescribed method for doing so has been outlined in Cameron and Quinn (2005). The process consists of eight steps which we describe briefly below.

1.   Diagnose the organization's current culture by completing the OCAI
Identify individuals in the organization who have a perspective on the organization's culture and who will be charged with implementing any

change efforts that are implemented. Once individual scores on the OCAI have been generated by this group, have those individuals meet together to generate a consensual view of the current organization's culture. The discussion that creates this consensus profile is the most important part of the exercise. Do not average or trade points, but reach consensus by exploring and discussing in depth all points of view.

2.   Diagnose the organization's desired future culture if the organization is to achieve its most optimistic aspirations

Repeat the process of having individuals complete the OCAI and reach consensus on the preferred culture. Collectively determine what the future culture must be like if the organization is to achieve spectacular performance and be the benchmark organization in its industry or sector.

Figure 7.3 shows the organizational culture plots of one organization that wanted to become engaged in the process of culture change. It shows major differences between the current organizational culture and the

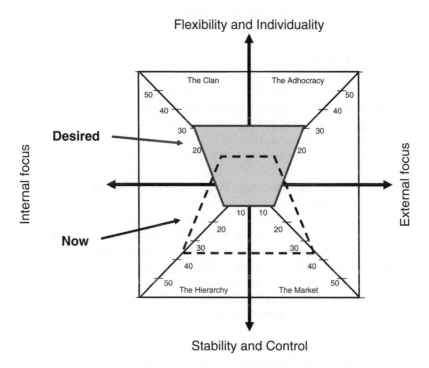

Figure 7.3   An example of an organization's current culture and preferred future culture

preferred culture needed in the future. Using that profile, the next steps of the process are undertaken.

3. Identify deep meaning

Having identified the discrepancies between current and preferred cultures, individuals should engage in an exercise to identify the implications or the meaning of the proposed cultural changes. That is, individuals answer two questions for each of the four quadrants in the Competing Values Framework: What does it mean to change? What doesn't it mean to change?

For example, in Figure 7.3, the organization would like to increase an emphasis on the Create culture and decrease the emphasis on the Compete culture. What it means to increase in the Create quadrant may entail, for example, more recognition of employee's innovative ideas or more tolerance for first-time mistakes. What it doesn't mean is to abandon procedures or to tolerate unnecessary risks. What it means to decrease emphasis in the Compete quadrant is to stop driving toward bottom-line numbers at all costs or to stop rewarding only measurable results. What it doesn't mean is to abandon an emphasis on customers or miss profit goals.

4. Tell core stories

Since organizational culture is best communicated through stories, identify incidents or illustrations in the company that characterize the new organizational culture. Provide an emotional as well as a cognitive picture of what the organization is striving to become. Capture a right-brain image of what the desired culture would look like by recounting a true incident where attributes of that desired culture were displayed in the past.

5. Identify strategic action steps that need to be put into place to achieve culture change

This process is often enhanced by asking questions such as: What should we do more of? What should we begin anew? What should we stop doing? Identifying ways to generate the needed social and financial support, ways to overcome anticipated resistance, ways to generate comitment to the new strategy, ways to measure progress and achievement, and ways to communicate the strategy to the rest of the organization all are necessary steps in the process of strategic implementation.

6. Identify immediate small wins

In order to get the ball rolling toward culture change, a small wins process should be put into place. This is a process of identifying something easy to change, changing it, and then publicizing it. Then selecting a second thing easy to change, changing it, and publicizing it. These kinds of small, incremental steps toward the ultimate objective of culture change create momentum, foster the image of progress, reduce resistance, get the process underway immediately, and create a bandwagon effect with members of the organization who need to be brought along.

7. Identify the leadership implications of the culture change

When the culture change takes place successfully, what kinds of leaders will need to be in place to manage in it? What will it take to get leaders prepared for that change? What changes should be made in the hiring and promotion decisions? What leadership development activities need to be put into place? What leadership competencies will be different from what is typical now in the organization?

8. Develop metrics, measures, and milestones

In order to maintain accountability, and in order to ensure that evidence is produced that change is and has occurred, metrics must be developed. Metrics are indicators or criteria of the culture change. Measures are processes or devices that assess the change. Milestones are timelines and benchmarks that answer the question: 'When will we have achieved successful change?' All three factors need to be developed for successful culture change to occur.

These eight steps, in sum, are designed to help leaders implement the process of organizational culture change. They ensure that the organization is clear from the outset about its current culture, why change is needed, how culture change will occur, and what the future organizational culture will look like. Unsuccessful culture change efforts are almost always impeded by an absence of a framework and a common language for how to address culture change. The Competing Values Framework overcomes that major obstacle and provides an effective process as well as an effective methodology for addressing this highly complicated issue.

MERGER SUCCESS AND CULTURE PROFILES

One additional implication of the Competing Values Framework and organizational culture relates to the issue of merging organizational cultures or acquiring an organization with a different culture. It has been well documented in academic research that the majority of company acquisitions do not succeed. That is, most mergers or acquisitions do not succeed in creating wealth for the acquiring firm's shareholders (see, for example,

Boquist et al., 2000). The reason is that the merging firms do not produce the efficiencies and cost savings projected to result from the merger, so that the acquiring firm's shareholders do not earn an adequate return on the price they pay for the target company.

Two primary reasons have been cited for the failure of most mergers: (1) the price paid by the acquiring firm was too high, and (2) the cultures of the two firms are not compatible and cannot be fused. Cultural incompatibilities result in tension, inefficiency, wasted energy, and ineffective performance. A great deal of research has been focused on trying to accurately specify the financial value of firms and the appropriate price that should be paid when they are acquired (see, for example, the summary in Boquist et al., 2000). On the other hand, there is a dearth of research on cultural incompatibility, and little is known about what to look for in selecting compatible cultures with which to merge. Very few instruments exist to accurately assess an organization's culture, and almost nothing has been done to date on trying to predict merger and acquisition success based on cultural compatibility.

Our own research using the Competing Values Framework has examined cultural compatibility and merger success, and the findings are notable. In brief, one of our analyses examined about 40 firms that had merged over the last five years. Using the Capital Asset Pricing Model to identify the firm's expected shareholder returns, we divided these companies into three groups depending on their actual realized returns. Merged companies that performed more than 20 percent higher than was expected were considered to be successful. Merged companies that performed more than 20 percent lower than was expected were considered unsuccessful. Merged companies with performance between −20 percent and +20 percent were considered to be neutral. In this analysis, in other words, we compared the over-achievers to the under-achievers, and we ignored those in the middle. Eight successful companies and six unsuccessful companies were compared on the basis of their cultural profiles one year after their merger had been announced (Cameron and Mora, 2002).

Using discriminant analysis, we were able to predict with a high degree of accuracy which mergers would succeed and which would fail based on the cultural compatibility of the merging companies. Based on culture data alone gathered with the OCAI, without consideration of industry type or firm size, we were able to correctly classify six of the eight successful companies and five of the six unsuccessful companies. The predictive capability of the findings, based on organizational cultures of successful and unsuccessful firms, was significant at the .034 level (or in 34 times out of 1000, our predictions would be incorrect).

The point of this research is to illuminate the power of cultural assessment in the prediction of organizational success when different organizational cultures are combined. The results are more complicated than merely a one-for-one match among quadrants on the Competing Values Framework, but the predictive power of the framework is quite remarkable. Having only information about culture – not industry, not size, not product life, not market share, not employee turnover rates, not competitive positioning in the industry, not any other type of data – successful mergers and acquisitions can be predicted by knowing about organizational culture congruence.

ADDITIONAL ASSESSMENT INSTRUMENTS – OUTCOMES AND CHANGE STRATEGIES

Although we have conducted extensive research on the leadership competencies instrument and the organizational culture instrument discussed above, other instruments have also been developed to assess aspects of organizational functioning and performance using the Competing Values Framework. That is, the framework has been used to create measurement devices – used in a variety of organizations for their own unique purposes – that assess a variety of other aspects of organizational operations. Two such instruments are summarized here by way of example, and the authors can be contacted for information regarding these and other instruments.

We provide an outline of two instruments below, a measure of organizational outcomes and a measure of strategies for organizational change. At this writing, these two instruments do not have the same empirical support that the competencies and culture instruments do, but theoretically they are expected to follow the same pattern of congruence that is typical of the competencies and culture instruments. That is, when the approach to organizational change is congruent with the outcomes being pursued, and when those two factors are congruent with organizational culture and leadership competencies, it is expected that performance will be significantly enhanced. As described above, this congruence principle has been empirically supported on a consistent basis when studying the Competing Values Framework for more than two decades.

Outcomes

The instrument assessing outcomes is designed to answer the question: 'What is the organization trying to accomplish, and how is it performing?' The instrument produces a map of an organization's current orientation toward performance as well as its relative level of performance compared to other organizations. The instrument also provides a profile of the kinds of performance the organization would like to achieve if it were to accomplish its highest aspirations in the future. This assessment permits comparisons between an organization's performance and its industry average – or the average competitor organization – as well as to the kind of performance that will be required to succeed in the future.

Because it is based on the Competing Values Framework, the Performance Outcomes Assessment helps create a common language among employees and gives them an easy way to understand desired results. It provides a way to discuss the culture, organizational capabilities, management competencies, personal orientation issues, and change processes that can all be used to bring about the desired results. Aligning these various aspects of organizational change and improvement is facilitated by having all instruments based on the same theoretical framework.

This instrument is completed by dividing 100 points among four alternatives depending on how similar the description is to the organization being studied. The assessment uses this ipsative scoring method to demonstrate that trade-offs are always necessary in organizations. No individual and no organization can do everything with equal emphasis. The primary consideration in responding to these items is to rate the organization in terms of how it is performing relative to the industry average or, stated another way, compared to the typical organization with which it competes.

Here are the items in the Performance Outcomes Assessment Instrument. Scoring keys, plotting profiles, and comparison data are available from the authors, although as a result of the copyright restriction associated with this instrument, permission is required to administer it.

Item 1
A. We excel in retaining our best employees.
B. We excel in launching new products or services.
C. We excel in acquiring financial revenues.
D. We excel in our percent of on-time deliveries.

Item 2
A. We excel in our employee morale.
B. We excel in the number of new sources of revenue created.
C. We excel in the amount of cash we have on hand (cash flow).
D. We excel in internal cost savings.

Item 3
A. We excel in the number of top quality people we have hired.
B. We excel in the return on investment from our innovations.

C. We excel in profitability (Return on Assets).
D. We excel in our improvements regarding error or defect rates.

Item 4
A. We excel in our improvement in stress-related health care costs.
B. We excel in obtaining revenues from new products or services.
C. We excel in increasing shareholder value (EVA).
D. We excel in our reduction in redundancy and waste.

Item 5
A. We excel in getting a return on investment from our in training and education.
B. We excel in increasing our brand recognition.
C. We excel in reducing our cycle time.
D. We excel in increasing our stock price.

Item 6
A. We excel in reducing grievances and complaints from employees.
B. We excel in obtaining growth in sales.
C. We excel in our overall performance ranking in the industry.
D. We excel in quality improvement.

Examples of the types of outcomes that are relevant in each of the Competing Values Framework quadrants are outlined in Figure 7.4. Whereas most organizations do a reasonably good job of assessing criteria in the bottom two quadrants, few are as systematic and rigorous in assessing outcomes in the top two quadrants. As discussed in Chapter 6, solid evidence is available suggesting that performance is higher when clear measurements and strategies are anchored in each of the four quadrants.

Change Strategies

An assessment instrument measuring change strategies helps create a map of the strategies used in an organization when planning and implementing change. Every organization is continuously engaged in the change process – whether by choice or because the environment demands it. The trouble is, most change initiatives do not achieve their desired outcome, at least partly because the strategies used to plan and implement change are under-developed, non-systematic, or off-target. This instrument helps identify the strategies for planning and implementing change that are most effective, based on their congruence with style, culture, competencies, and performance outcomes.

COLLABORATE	CREATE
• Employee retention rate • Measures of employee morale • Number of top quality people attracted and hired • Percent improvement in stress-related health care costs • Return on investment in training/education • Reduction in internal grievances/complaints	• The number of new products or services launched • Number of new sources of revenue • Return on investment in innovation • Revenues derived from new products or services • Measures of brand recognition • Total growth in sales
• Percent of on-time deliveries • Total internal cost savings • Improvement on error or defect rate • Percent reduction in redundancy or waste • Measures of reduced cycle time • Measures of quality improvement	• Total revenue • Amount of cash on hand (cash flow) • Profitability (return on assets) • Shareholder value (EVA) • Stock price • Overall performance ranking in the industry
CONTROL	COMPETE

Figure 7.4   Examples of performance outcomes in each quadrant

Each organization possesses its own unique approach to planning and executing change, of course, but this instrument highlights the core approaches and inclinations. Because it is based on the Competing Values Framework, the assessment helps create a common language among employees providing them with an easy way to discuss how to effectively achieve the desired results. The instrument helps members of the organization come to an agreement about effective change strategies as well as leading them through a process for effectively planning and implementing change.

The same process is used to complete this instrument as is used to complete the outcomes instrument, that is, by dividing 100 points among the various alternatives. Again, scoring keys, plotting profiles, and comparison data are available from the authors, although as a result of the copyright restriction associated with this instrument, permission is required to administer it.

1. **Change initiatives tend to materialize from our analysis of:**
A. Feedback from our employees
B. Emerging external opportunities
C. The behavior of our competitors
D. Internal process measurements

2. **During the process of planning for change, we assess:**
A. Our people's willingness to change
B. The interests of our external stake holders
C. The payoffs of the potential change
D. Our technical capacity to make the change

3. **During the planning process we focus on:**
A. Preparing to alter the human culture
B. Developing a strategic vision
C. Making the business case for change
D. Developing clear plans and budgets

4. **At the outset of our implementation of change, we emphasize that change leaders have:**
A. High levels of trust in their people
B. An ability to adapt quickly
C. An intense performance focus
D. Logical, step by step processes to follow

5. **During the implementation process our senior managers:**
A. Model the new behaviors required by the change
B. Use powerful symbols to highlight a meaningful vision
C. Communicate that the change is a top priority by rewarding success and correcting failures
D. Carefully monitor the costs of change

6. **During the implementation process we:**
A. Listen to the problems encountered by our people
B. Stay flexible and adapt to feedback from multiple sources
C. Persist in the face of resistance or adversity
D. Minimize disruption to our workflow

Examples of the major approaches to organizational change are briefly summarized in Figure 7.5. Again, these strategies may not fit precisely with the requirements of each change effort, but they highlight the importance of a well-rounded change initiative.

COLLABORATE	CREATE
Our initiatives often emerge from analysing employee feedback. In planning change we assess our people's readiness and recognize the need to alter the human culture. We emphasize high mutual trust for employees and the modeling of the behaviors needed from the workforce. During implementation we listen to the problems encountered by our people.	Our initiatives often emerge from identifying external opportunities. In planning change, we assess the interests of our external stake holders. We develop a strategic vision for change. We emphasize flexibility and the ability to adapt quickly and to use powerful symbols to communicate the meaningfulness of the change. During implementation we monitor the feedback from the market.
Our change initiatives often emerge from the analysis of internal process measurements. In planning change we assess our technical capacity to make change and develop careful plans and budgets to guide the process. We emphasize a step by step process and to carefully monitor the costs of the change. During implementation we strive to minimize the disruption to the workflow	Our change initiatives often emerge from the analysis of competitor behavior. In planning change we identify the potential payoffs and make the business case for the change. We emphasize an intense performance focus and using reward systems to show that change in a top priority. During implementation we expect to persist in the face of resistance and adversity.
CONTROL	COMPETE

Figure 7.5   Core elements in organizational change

SUMMARY

In sum, the Competing Values Framework can be extremely useful to leaders in identifying a variety of personal and organizational attributes, all designed to reinforce the importance of congruence. When the outcomes being pursued are aligned with leadership capabilities, change strategies, organizational culture, and personal orientations, organizations tend toward high performance and positive deviance. High performance is a product of the alignment among these various strategies, competencies, and attributes (Whetten and Cameron, 2005). In particular, because organizational culture has been such an amorphous concept, and a difficult feature of organizations to measure, the cultural diagnosis instrument (OCAI), along with a culture change process, is one of the most widely used and beneficial tools for organizations faced with the need for cultural change. This assessment device, along with its companion instruments, can be helpful tools for leaders engaged in organizational improvement. The Competing Values Framework, in other words, has proven to be a very robust tool for enhancing value in a variety of areas.

8. Applying leadership levers for organizational change

Changes in organizational culture, as identified in the previous chapter, require changes in organizational strategy, tactics, competencies, and relationships. The basic values and orientations of organizations are operationalized by these various manifestations of culture. Consequently, as leaders are faced with an opportunity to implement changes in their organizations, they require a portfolio of tools and techniques that will help them lead change successfully. To effectively implement both broad and deep change – as in the case of culture change – as well as small, incremental changes – as in the case of daily adjustments and modifications – leaders need a portfolio of options available to them. Providing a few such options is our purpose in this chapter.

We provide some tools and techniques that have proven to be successful in helping organizations implement value adding change. We have selected just one tool or technique for each quadrant simply to illustrate the kinds of levers that leaders may utilize as they implement change in their organizations. The main emphasis of each of these tools or techniques resides in a single quadrant in the Competing Values Framework. That is, the major objective of each tool or technique is to change the organization in one particular quadrant. However, we also illustrate that the effective implementation of each change lever is possible only when all the quadrants in the model are utilized. Our intent is not to be comprehensive or thorough in our explanations, nor are the four change levers discussed here necessarily the most important in every organizational setting. We don't propose that they are universally useful in every organizational change endeavor. Rather, we highlight certain tools and techniques that we have utilized ourselves, that we have studied in our research, and that we have observed in especially successful organizations.

LEVERS OF CHANGE IN THE COLLABORATE QUADRANT

One of the well-researched findings in organization and management science since the 1960s concludes that when environments are predictable and stable, organizations can function as routine, controlled, mechanistic units. Under such conditions, employees can be expected to follow rules and procedures and to engage in standardized, formalized behavior. Managers can maintain control and issue top-down mandates regarding the strategy and direction to be pursued by the organization.

However, the modern business environment is more accurately described using terms such as 'hyper-turbulence,' 'complexity,' 'speed,' 'competition,' 'unpredictability,' and 'threatening.' Under such conditions, prescriptions for organizational effectiveness call for a flexible, autonomous, self-governing workforce, rather than one that relies on senior management for direction and control. Less-centralized decision making, less top-down control, and less-directive leadership are all prescribed as prerequisites for high-performing organizations.

Our own research has shown, however, that instead of becoming adaptable, flexible, autonomous, and self-managing, organizations in rapidly changing, complex environments tend to develop the opposite characteristics. They tend to become less flexible, less adaptable, less autonomous, less self-managing, and, instead, become more rigid, more resistive, more secretive and more defensive when they face turbulence and change (Cameron, 1998; Cameron et al., 1987a; Cameron et al., 1987b).

How can organizations in the conditions of uncertainty and turbulence develop the prescribed characteristics for effectiveness – that is, how can they become adaptable, flexible, autonomous, and self-managing? If people and systems become more rigid and resistant in uncertain times, how can they ever perform effectively?

One answer is the implementation of empowerment – a Collaborate quadrant strategy. If organizations have developed the capability to empower the workforce, the inertia that drives organizations toward rigidity and dysfunction is counteracted by a committed, self-motivated workforce, and the organization becomes more effective, even during trying times. Empowerment is a key to unlocking the potential of a successful workforce in an era of chaotic change and escalating competitive conditions.

To empower means to enable, to help organization members develop a sense of self-confidence, to help people overcome feelings of powerlessness or helplessness. It refers to energizing people to take action, mobilizing intrinsic motivation to accomplish a task. Empowered people not only possess the wherewithal to accomplish something, but they also think of themselves as more capable and confident than they did before they were empowered.

Empirical research has identified five key dimensions of effective organizational empowerment (Spreitzer, 1992; Mishra, 1992). The presence of these five attributes is strongly associated with enhanced productivity, satisfaction, employee retention, profitability, and shareholder value (Quinn and Spreitzer, 1997). That is, creating value by focusing on the Collaborate quadrant is facilitated by engendering these five attributes in the organization's employees. Effective empowerment means that organization members experience five core mind-sets: (1) a sense of self-efficacy, (2) a sense of self-determination, (3) a sense of personal consequence, (4) a sense of meaning, and (5) a sense of trust.

Specifically, self-efficacy means that an organization's employees possess the capability and the competence to perform a task successfully. Empowered people not only feel competent, they feel confident that they can perform adequately. They feel a sense of personal mastery and believe they can learn and grow to meet new challenges (Bandura, 1997).

Empowered organizations also create a sense of self-determination in employees, which means a feeling of having a choice. People feel self-determined when they can voluntarily and intentionally involve themselves in tasks rather than being forced or prohibited from involvement. They have a measure of personal freedom and autonomy, which leads to a sense of responsibility for and ownership of their own work. They are able to take initiative on their own accord, make independent decisions, and try out new ideas.

Empowered people also have a sense of personal control over outcomes. They believe that they can make a difference by influencing the environment in which they work or the outcomes being produced. Personal consequence is the conviction that actions taken can influence collective results. A sense of personal consequence, then, refers to a perception of having impact.

Similarly, empowered organizations foster a sense of meaning among employees. This indicates that people value the purpose, goals, and vision of the organization. Their own ideals and standards are congruent with those of the organization, so they believe in and care about what they produce. Their work tends to be infused with a sense of purpose, passion, energy, and enthusiasm.

Finally, empowerment relies on a sense of trust. People are confident that they will be treated fairly and equitably. The ultimate outcome of their actions will be justice and goodness as opposed to harm or hurt. Usually, this means they have confidence that those holding authority or power positions will not harm or injure them, and that they will be treated respectfully and impartially.

Ironically, most large organizations engender the opposite dynamics in their people because bureaucracy encourages dependency and submission. Rules, routines, and traditions define what can be done, stifling and supplanting initiative and discretion. In such circumstances, the formal organization needs a tool or technique that can be applied to alter these dysfunctional dynamics. In most large organizations, in other words, empowerment is an especially needed lever of change.

Research by a variety of scholars has produced a set of prescriptions for fostering empowerment in organizations (Cameron, 2005b). Eleven that are commonly implemented by effective organizations are listed in Figure 8.1. Their purpose, collectively, is to enhance in the organization's employees a sense of competence, choice, impact, value, and security.

One of the most important values of the Competing Values Framework, as mentioned in earlier chapters, is to organize sets of disparate or complex phenomena. In this case, the framework helps identify how effective empowerment is reliant on activities in each of the four quadrants. Adequately achieving a change in empowerment, in other words, depends on complementary as well as contradictory activities. Figure 8.1 summarizes the commonly prescribed strategies for enhancing empowerment.

The relationships between these prescriptions and the five dimensions of empowerment are summarized in Table 8.1. The point is that when these 11 activities are fostered in organizations, empowerment improves and,

COLLABORATE **Provide support** (Institutionalize encouragement, feedback, praise, reassurance, and recognition events.) **Form teams** (Engender opportunities for formalized collaboration across boundaries, in self-managing teams, and in cases when participation brings about buy-in.) **Provide modeling** (Provide examples of successful performance, mentors, and coaches.)	CREATE **Articulate vision** (Create a picture of the desired future with word pictures and superlative language as well as specific targets.) **Arouse positive emotions** (Maintain a positive, lighthearted, energetic, and/or passionate climate in the organization to infuse energy into others.)
CONTROL **Provide mastery experiences** (Break apart large, complex tasks into small and simple tasks, use a small wins strategy, and celebrate incremental progress.) **Provide information** (Continuously share need-to-know as well as nice-to-know information to all who are affected, along with providing access to information and its sources.) **Provide resources** (Provide adequate time, space, and financial resources, including technical and administrative support.) **Create confidence** (Exhibit reliability, consistency, fairness, equity, personal expertise and personal concern.)	COMPETE **Specify goals** (Identify SMART goals that are specific, measurable, aligned, reachable, and time-bound, along with measures and accountability for success.) **Connect to outcomes** (Provide direct access to customers, authority to resolve problems on the spot, task identity, and clarity about the effects of work.)

Figure 8.1   Prescriptions for enhancing value through empowerment

Table 8.1   Relationships between activities and empowerment dimensions

---

Self Efficacy (competence)
- Provide mastery experiences
- Provide modeling
- Connect to outcomes

Self-Determination (choice)
- Articulate vision
- Specify goals
- Provide information

Personal Consequence (impact)
- Connect to outcomes
- Provide resources
- Provide mastery experiences

Meaningfulness (value)
- Articulate vision
- Arouse positive emotions
- Articulate vision

Trust (security)
- Create confidence
- Form teams
- Provide information

---

consequently, so do related indicators of success such as productivity, customer satisfaction, employee retention, and profitability (Spreitzer, 1992; Mishra, 1992).

A good example of the positive results that come from an empowered workforce is the Rocky Flats project mentioned in Chapter 1. CH2MHill, an engineering and environmental company, obtained a contract in 1995 to clean up a nuclear arsenal that contained hundreds of buildings and thousands of acres of radioactively polluted land. For 50 years CH2MHill had been producing the triggers for nuclear weapons. The original budget provided by the federal government to close and clean-up the site was $36 billion, and the estimate for completing the job was 70 years. The project was actually completed in 2005, 60 years early, and at a cost savings of $30 billion. As described in detail by Cameron and Lavine (2006), among the keys to success associated with this remarkable achievement was the empowerment of not only the workforce but of multiple constituencies associated with the project. Two quotations – one from a senior elected official and the other from a senior manager – illustrate the central role of empowerment in achieving this remarkable success (Cameron and Lavine, 2006).

I think there are some general principles here that are really important. One is, you can't make decisions in secret when people's future and their welfare are involved. They want to know what is going on, they want to have some kind of say, and they want to know that they're being heard. So, being open in public is very important. Second is bringing in the leadership of all of the local communities as well as the state and the federal leadership. Ultimately the money is going to come from the federal government, so they need to be involved. Nothing was going to get done if we had people filing lawsuits, or if you had local communities saying 'Not in my backyard.' A third thing is that people will focus on solving problems if you empower them to do it, if you entrust them to solve it. They may fight bitterly, but if somebody is standing there saying, 'Solve the problem, I know you can do it,' they'll do it. People really do rise to the occasion . . . So, my top advice is to make sure that your various constituencies are heard. Make sure they have a say in what is in their best interest. (Senior elected government official)

An extremely important and often overlooked major sea change had to do with our relationship with the workforce, and specifically with the steel workers, the guards unions, and the trade unions. They're the ones who do the work, and they're the ones who built up the nuclear weapons arsenal. They're the ones who for 40 years served a very patriotic purpose. In the early part of the 1990s they were kind of cast off as having very little value in the whole process. In the mid-1990s we started to bring them back in and made them part of the process. This was through the integrated safety management program, the ISMS program, the new contracts, and the work planning. To have them part of that process and to tailor the contracts, the work agreements, and to make them part of the success was absolutely essential. (Senior manager)

What these quotations illustrate is that in conditions of major change and required improvement, empowerment as a tool in the Collaborate quadrant is essential. Not only did the workforce need to become empowered, but other external constituency groups were also empowered to take action to assist with the clean-up of the country's most polluted site. Table 8.1 is a summary of several key levers that can be used to enhance empowerment among employees.

LEVERS OF CHANGE IN THE CONTROL QUADRANT

We have found that many organizations desire to decrease their emphasis on the Control quadrant as they contemplate culture change. Control and hierarchy are often viewed with a negative lens, and avoidance of this quadrant is more typical of the average leader than desiring an enhanced emphasis. On the other hand, no organization can succeed unless a solid foundation of carefully designed systems and processes serve as a basis for operation.

Achieving high levels of quality (i.e., zero defects and timeliness of delivery) depends on doing things right, the first time, every time, anywhere. Eliminating waste, redundancy, and errors is a product of succeeding in the Control quadrant. No company is ISO 9000 certified, for example, without having superb Control quadrant processes in place.

One of the most important tools for enhancing performance in the Control quadrant is 'process management.' This technique aims to add value to an organization by getting processes under control and by making them more efficient and effective. By processes we mean the methods and procedures used in organizations to achieve outcomes and objectives. Processes refer to the *ways* things get done. They might include the manufacturing methods, employee evaluation methods, accounting methods, strategy setting methods, customer monitoring methods, and so on.

One of the highest rates of demise among small entrepreneurial firms comes when they are required to move from a run-and-gun approach to business – led by a creative founder and a few pioneering colleagues – to a stable, predictable, and efficient operation. This necessary shift toward the Control quadrant and toward process management provides the reliability that allows the organization to grow past infancy. Moreover, process management is required any time organizations are faced with high costs, unpredictable outcomes, or slow production. Ask almost anyone in the automotive industry and they will tell you that American automobile makers are still a step behind the best Japanese automobile makers in process management. The differential in profitability, market share, and company growth can be directly attributed to competency in process management. In the modern environment when timeliness is a significant predictor of customer satisfaction and profitability for most companies, speed of production and rapidity of service delivery separates winning organizations from losing organizations, and they depend on process management.

A good example of value creation through process management is the breakthrough in manufacturing efficiency achieved by Toyota in the 1970s and 1980s through a dramatic reduction in changeover time. In the 1960s, the changeover time – the time it takes for the factory to change the manufacturing layout and assembly equipment to deal with a different model – was a few hours and about the same for American and Japanese manufacturers. However, Toyota was able to reduce this to just a few minutes by the 1970s, gaining an enormous competitive advantage over American manufacturers. While others have now almost caught up and all major manufacturers have changeover times that span just seconds, Toyota still enjoys a significant cost advantage over competitors.

In brief, process management is based on the assumption that processes are the key attributes of the organizational design, rather than technologies or structures. Processes are measured and monitored, so that the way things get done is measured as well as what gets done. Processes directly related to customers take priority and are the first to be improved. This means that constant feedback from internal and external customers is sought regarding not only what they received but also the processes by which it was produced and delivered. A specific champion owns and is held accountable for each process in the organization.

Improvements in process management are guided by several well-known principles:

Customers

Focus on business processes that are strategically important. In particular, analyse and improve processes that affect total customer cost and satisfaction. Focus on what customers want, not on what the unit may want, by reducing time, space, investment, and complexity. Ask the question, does the customer care about this, or will any customer pay for this activity? Move resources and decision making to the point where 'customer work' is being done. This requires providing decision support, management controls, and adequate amounts of authority.

Boundarylessness

The best opportunities for improvement are often found at the boundaries (the white space) of the organization such as across work groups, functional, location, or business boundaries. Jack Welch, the former CEO at General Electric, adopted as a mantra that the firm would become boundaryless. This means that unit boundaries could not stand in the way of efficient processes in whatever domain of activity. The question is, do the organization's processes foster toll booths, sign-offs, clearances, slow-downs, and red tape, or do they facilitate smooth flowing, efficient, boundaryless activity?

Root Causes

Measure and document errors, delays, redundancies, and costs and trace them back to their root causes. For example, at Toyota Motor a rule of five why's exists. That is, processes are often challenged with supervisors or employees asking 'why? why? why?' five times to get at the root success factors as well as the root causes of error. The processes are then redesigned so problems don't repeat themselves and so the need to do more root cause analysis is also eliminated. The question is, what are the root causes, the key explanatory factors, the real reasons why the results occurred? What can be fixed so the issue never arises again?

Leanness

Lean companies are conscious of excess, waste, redundancy, and rework. Eliminating multiple sources of fat – for example knowledge fat (too much unused knowledge), training fat (too much time in unproductive training), career fat (self-aggrandizing behavior that deflects energy away from collective effort) – is typical of lean organizations. Opportunities to get lean are especially present in the support and staff services. Getting lean means to eliminate waste, delay, inventories, work-in-process, and process variation in the service side of the organization. Shifting organizational energy from detection and inspection to prevention and anticipation, and ensuring that process redesign is an iterative activity, not a one-time change, are also principles of leanness.

By way of illustration, Table 8.2 summarizes some differences between the way most organizations make and sell products (e.g., cars, televisions, computers) compared to lean production processes (Liker, 2005).

Notice from Table 8.2 that processes in traditional organizations tend to be limited to the Control quadrant – an emphasis on specialists, limited interactions, and remaining internally focused. Lean production processes, on the other hand, cross boundaries and rely of activities that

Table 8.2   Lean production processes

Process	Traditional	Lean production
Employees	Specialists	Generalists
Sequencing	Pass-along to specialists	Interchangeable members
Supplier involvement	After design	Before design
Contract awarding	Low cost bid	Lifetime relationship
Information	Little shared (secretive)	Total sharing (open books)
Scheduling	Buffers smooth production	No safety net (perfection)
Sales	Customer comes to dealer	Dealer goes to customer
Promotion	Competency in specialty	Expand competency base
Source of data	From customer	From family of customer
Objectives	Sales and profit	Lifelong loyalty
Contacts with customers	Infrequent	Frequent
Sales philosophy	Sell what is made	Make what is sold
Purchase experience	In the company's store	On line at home

reside in all four quadrants of the Competing Values Framework – for example, total sharing (Collaborate quadrant), expanding the competency base (Create quadrant), and frequent customer contact (Compete quadrant). That is, even though lean production is clearly a Control quadrant phenomenon, it relies on each of the other quadrants to be effectively implemented.

In other words, to be effectively implemented, process management involves each of the quadrants in the Competing Values Framework. To illustrate this principle, consider the three simple steps that are involved in process management – first, process *assessment* (Figure 8.2); second, process *analysis* (Figure 8.3); and third, process *redesign* (Figure 8.4).

The first step, process assessment, aims to identify the processes that are currently being used for achieving an outcome. Figure 8.2 summarizes the steps.

The objective of process assessment is to identify the sequence of tasks, activities, and individuals that creates an output for a customer. Once the process has been identified and mapped, process analysis occurs. The objective of process analysis is to identify a better way to perform the sequence of activities identified in the process assessment step. Again, each of the quadrants in the Competing Values Framework are utilized to effectively implement this activity, as summarized in Figure 8.3.

COLLABORATE	CREATE
1. Form a team consisting of cross-functional and cross unit representatives. 4. Reach consensus in the team regarding the crucial activities involved in the process.	
CONTROL	**COMPETE**
3. Walk the process. For example, follow a customer order from the time it is received in the organization until the customer receives and pays for the product or service. Document each step. 5. Create a process map of the process as it currently exists.	2. Talk with internal and external customers about the process to identify expectations, problems, and suggestions.

Figure 8.2   Steps in process assessment

COLLABORATE	CREATE
1. Focus on the inputs, outputs, and exchanges between different individuals and different units. 3. Identify incremental improvements to the process by involving individuals engaged in the process.	5. Re-engineer the process. Start from scratch and re-think the entire set of activities. 6. Construct an ideal or 'should be' process map by simplifying, eliminating non-value-adding activities, and by removing redundancies, excess costs, disconnects, and unmeasured activities.
CONTROL	**COMPETE**
2. Find out how others perform the same process by benchmarking; borrow and copy ideas.	4. Ask customers about their ideas to redesign the process. Use focus groups and on-site conversations.

Figure 8.3   Steps in process analysis

COLLABORATE	CREATE
1. Involve the entire team in mapping the new idealized process. Ensure buy-in through participation.	3. Try out, and experiment with, new processes on a practice-field or in a pilot project before applying it organization-wide.
CONTROL	**COMPETE**
2. Establish benchmark measures and an on-going monitoring system to keep track of improvements.	4. Assess the impact of the changed processes on customers and on the organization's outcomes.

Figure 8.4   Steps in process redesign

Process analysis allows the organization to create a new plan or prototype for conducting a process in a different, more efficient way. The third and final step involves process redesign. The purpose of process redesign is to re-create the process so that it is faster, less expensive, more efficient, more enjoyable, and produces higher quality than the previous process. Figure 8.4 summarizes the key steps in process redesign.

Most organizations have engaged in some kind of process management activity, but many organizations do not succeed because processes are too narrowly defined and too narrowly managed. They focus almost exclusively on measuring, monitoring, tightening, restraining, and standardizing. While these activities are important, the Competing Values Framework makes clear that a broader approach must be taken for process management to be complete. Many organizations have dramatically reduced set-up time (Ford Motor), product assembly time (Thomasville Furniture), error rates (Dana Corporation), and timeliness of client services (Citibank) by improving their process management activities. Effectively changing the Control quadrant, however, is clearly a challenge in all four quadrants of the framework.

LEVERS OF CHANGE IN THE CREATE QUADRANT

Whereas most individuals and organizations would like to be more effective in the Create quadrant, there are a number of inhibitors that keep organizations from being more innovative, visionary, flexible, and forward-thinking. Paradoxically, the more experience and success organizations have, the less able they are to solve problems in innovative ways and the more restrained they are in pursuing new, untested opportunities. Habitual and routinized activities, developed in organizations over time in order to cope with complexity and uncertainty, tend to hinder the organization's ability to be creative. Normal work patterns prescribe 'right' answers, analytic rules, and thinking boundaries, and experience in the marketplace often leads to 'proper' ways of doing things, specialized knowledge, and clear expectations of appropriate actions. Organizations thus lose the ability to experiment, improvise, or take detours. Consider the following example:

> If you place in a bottle half a dozen bees and the same number of flies, and lay the bottle down horizontally, with its base to the window, you will find that the bees will persist, till they die of exhaustion or hunger, in their endeavor to discover an issue through the glass; while the flies, in less than two minutes, will all have sallied forth through the neck on the opposite side. . . . It is [the bees'] love of light, it is their very intelligence, that is their undoing in this experiment. They evidently imagine that the issue from every prison must be where the light shines clearest; and they act in accordance, and persist in too logical an action. To them glass is a supernatural mystery they have never met in nature; they have had no experience of this suddenly impenetrable atmosphere; and the greater their intelligence, the more inadmissible, more incomprehensible, will the strange obstacle appear. Whereas the feather-brained flies, careless of logic as of the enigma of crystal, disregarding the call of the light, flutter wildly, hither and thither, meeting here the good fortune that often waits on the simple, who find salvation where the wiser will perish, necessarily end by discovering the friendly opening that restores their liberty to them. (Cameron, 2005a, pp. 164–5)

This illustration identifies a paradox inherent in improving organizational effectiveness in the Create quadrant. On the one hand, more past success and more experience may inhibit creativity and innovation. Like the bees in the story, organizations may not find solutions because the problem requires less 'educated' and more 'playful' approaches. On the other hand, as several researchers have found, certain tools and techniques, effectively applied, can lead organizations toward significant improvement in innovativeness. Three key strategies for enhancing an organization's ability to be innovative – Create quadrant activities – are discussed below. To explain them, we briefly describe two examples of value creation through innovation (see Cameron, 2005b).

During World War II, the British developed one of the best-kept military secrets of the war, a special radar detector based on a device called the magnetron. This radar was credited with turning the tide of battle in the war between Britain and Germany and helping the British withstand Hitler's Blitzkrieg. In 1940, Raytheon was one of several U.S. firms invited to produce magnetrons for the war effort. Unfortunately, the workings of magnetrons were not well understood even by sophisticated physicists. Among several firms that made magnetrons, few understood what made them work. A magnetron was tested, in those early days, by holding a neon tube next to it. If the neon tube got bright enough, the magnetron tube passed the test. In the process of conducting the test, the hands of the scientist holding the neon tube got warm. At the end of the war, the market for radar essentially dried up, and most firms stopped producing magnetrons. At Raytheon, however, a scientist named Percy Spencer began fooling around with magnetrons, trying to think of alternative uses for the devices. He was convinced that magnetrons could be used to cook food by using the heat produced in the neon tube. But Raytheon was in the defense business, and next to its two prize products – the Hawk and Sparrow missiles – cooking devices seemed odd and out of place. Not only that, but no one had any conception at that point of what eventually became the microwave oven. Innovation was clearly a necessity if the magnetron had any hope of a future in Raytheon's portfolio.

A second illustrative case is the well-known case of 3M's Post-it notes. Spence Silver had been assigned to work on a temporary project team within the company. The team was searching for new adhesives. Silver ended up producing a substance that failed all the conventional 3M tests for adhesives. It didn't stick. For five years, Silver went from department to department within the company trying to find someone interested in using his newly found substance in a product. Predictably, 3M showed little interest because the company's mission was to make adhesives that adhered ever more tightly. After four years the task force was disbanded, and team

COLLABORATE	CREATE
• Put people together. • Reward sponsors and mentors.	• Reward idea champions. • Reward rule breakers.
CONTROL	COMPETE
• Monitor. • Reward orchestrators.	• Pull people apart. • Prod.

Figure 8.5   Rules for fostering innovation

members were assigned to other projects. But Silver was still convinced that his substance was good for something. He just didn't know what. Innovation was needed in order to make Silver's non-sticking glue into something that would create value.

Three key rules that assist companies in producing the needed innovation are included in Figure 8.5 (see Cameron, 2005b).

Pull People Apart; Put People Together

Percy Spencer's magnetron project involved a consumer product closeted away from Raytheon's mainline business of missiles and other defense-contract work. Spence Silver's new glue resulted when a polymer adhesive task force was separated from 3M's normal activities. The Macintosh computer was developed by a task force taken outside the company and given space and time to work on an innovative computer. Many new ideas come from individuals being given time and resources and allowed to work apart from the normal activities of the organization. Establishing bullpens, practice fields, or incubating laboratories is as good a way to increase value in business as it has proven to be in athletics. Because most businesses are designed to produce the 10 000th part correctly or to service the 10 000th customer efficiently, they do not function well at producing the first part. That is why pulling people apart (separating them or providing them space) is often a prerequisite to innovation.

On the other hand, forming teams (putting people together) is almost always more productive than having people work by themselves. Innovation teams, however, should be characterized by certain attributes. For example, innovation increases markedly when 'devil's advocate' roles are present on the team, when a formal minority report is included in final recommendations, and when individuals assigned to work on a team have divergent backgrounds or views. Similarly, narrow-mindedness in groups (dubbed 'groupthink') is best overcome by establishing competing groups working on the same problem, by having outsiders participate in groups, by assigning a role of critical evaluator in the group, and by having groups made up of cross-functional participants. That is, by putting (different kinds of) people together, innovation is enhanced.

Innovativeness can be fostered, in other words, when individuals are placed in teams and when they are at least temporarily separated from the normal pressures of organizational life. Teams, however, are most effective at generating innovative ideas when they are characterized by attributes of minority influence, competition, heterogeneity, and interaction. In other words, create innovation by pulling them apart and putting them together.

Monitor and Prod

Neither Percy Spencer nor Spence Silver was allowed to work on their projects without accountability. Both men eventually had to report on the results they accomplished with their experimentation and imagination. At 3M, for example, people are expected to allocate 15 percent of their time away from company business to work on new, innovative ideas. They can even appropriate company materials and resources to work on them. However, individuals are always held accountable for their decisions. They need to show results for their 'play time.'

Holding people accountable for outcomes, in fact, is an important motivator for improved performance. Former Dana Corporation CEO Woody Morcott implemented a program, for example, that holds people accountable for innovation by requiring each person in the company to submit at least two suggestions for improvement each month. At least 70 percent of the new ideas must be implemented. Woody stole the idea during a visit to a Japanese company where he noticed workers huddled around a table scribbling notes on how some ideas for improvement might work. At Dana, this requirement is part of every person's job assignment. In addition to accountability, innovativeness is stimulated by what Gene Goodson, formerly president at Johnson Controls, called 'sharp-pointed prods.' After taking over the automotive group at that company, Goodson found that he could stimulate innovation by issuing certain mandates, such as: 'There will be no more forklift trucks allowed in any of our plants.' What makes this prod 'sharp-pointed' is that the plant has hundreds of thousands of square feet of floor space. The loading docks are on one side of the building, and tons of heavy raw materials are unloaded weekly and moved from the loading docks to work stations throughout the entire facility. The way it is done is with forklifts. The prod demanded that individuals working in the plant find ways to move the work stations closer to the raw materials, to move the unloading of the raw materials closer to the work stations, or to change the size and amounts of material being unloaded. The innovations that resulted from eliminating forklifts saved the company millions of dollars in materials handling and wasted time.

In summary, innovativeness is often fostered by holding people accountable for new ideas and by stimulating them with periodic prods. Frequently these sharp-pointed prods come from customers.

Reward Multiple Roles

The success of the sticky yellow notes at 3M illustrates the four key roles required in innovation creation. They include the idea champion (the person who comes up with innovative problem solutions), the sponsor or mentor (the person who helps provide the resources, environment, and encouragement for the idea champion to work on his or her idea), the orchestrator or facilitator (the person who brings together cross-functional groups and necessary political support to facilitate implementation of creative ideas), and the rule breaker (the person who goes beyond organizational boundaries and barriers to ensure success of the innovation). Each of these roles is present in most important innovations in organizations and all are illustrated by the Post-it note example below.

1. Spence Silver (idea champion and rule breaker) was fooling around with chemical configurations that the academic literature indicated wouldn't work, and he invented a glue that wouldn't stick. Silver spent years giving presentations to any audience at 3M that would listen, trying to pawn off his glue on some division that could find a practical application for it. Nobody was interested.
2. Henry Courtney and Roger Merrill (sponsors) developed a coating substance that allowed the glue to stick to one surface but not to others. This made it possible to produce a permanently temporary glue, that is, one that would peel off easily when pulled but would otherwise hang on forever.
3. Art Fry (idea champion and orchestrator) found a problem that fitted Spence Silver's solution. He found an application for the glue as a 'better bookmark' and as a note pad. No equipment existed at 3M to coat only a part of a piece of paper with the glue. Fry, therefore, carried 3M equipment and tools home to his own basement, where he designed and made his own machine to manufacture the forerunner of Post-it notes. He then brought together engineers, designers, production managers, and machinists to demonstrate the prototype machine and generate enthusiasm for manufacturing the product.

4.　Geoffrey Nicholson and Joseph Ramsey (sponsors and rule breakers) began marketing the product inside 3M. They also submitted the product to the standard 3M market tests. The product failed miserably. No one wanted to pay $1.00 for a pad of scratch paper. But Nicholson and Ramsey broke 3M rules by personally visiting test market sites and giving away free samples, and the consuming public became addicted.

Had 3M been interested only in recognizing, rewarding, and supporting idea champions – i.e., the people who came up with the new idea – Post-it notes would never have been developed. It is when organizations recognize the value of multiple roles that innovation is effectively achieved. And, once again these multiple roles represent the various quadrants in the Competing Values Framework. Specifically, idea champions and rule breakers emphasize the Create quadrant; sponsors emphasize the Compete quadrant; and orchestrators emphasize the Control quadrant.

In sum, the innovation process, as illustrated above, is a key lever for producing value in the Create quadrant. It is easy to see once again, however, that all four quadrants of the Competing Values Framework are needed if innovative change is to be successful.

LEVERS OF CHANGE IN THE COMPETE QUADRANT

The change lever we focus on in the Compete quadrant is sustaining shareholder value creation, usually measured as Economic Value Added (EVA) (see Thakor, 2000). As discussed in Chapters 2 and 6, creating value is the core mission of any organization, and, again, the creation of value is defined in an organization as:

Value created = *Benefits produced* minus *Direct costs* minus *Opportunity costs*

Usually 'benefits' are defined as revenues in for-profit organizations. 'Direct costs' are the expenses associated with producing the goods or services (such as equipment, raw materials, wages, taxes). 'Opportunity costs' refer to the amount that could have been earned if the money had been used elsewhere (say, invested in some other way). So, for publicly-traded companies, value creation is linked to the financial returns the company delivers to its shareholders. In not-for-profit organizations, it may be the services provided which satisfy the needs of clients or customers. The only reason organizations survive over the long run is because they produce sustained economic value. That is, they produce more than they consume. The value of the outcomes they generate exceeds the value of the resources they use in generating them. When comparing what they get versus what they give, value creating organizations give more than they get.

To repeat, creating value is the core mission of any organization. Organizations that maximize value are those that achieve the goals expected of them by shareholders, sponsors, or stakeholders. It is clear, unfortunately, that sustained value creation does not happen consistently. Ron Miller of the Walt Disney Company lost his job as CEO in 1984 despite the company's outstanding brand quality and Miller's family ties to Walt Disney himself. IBM fired John Akers as CEO in 1993 and replaced him with Louis Gerstner, despite the fact that the company was still a dominant force in the computer industry. In these cases, the reason for the firing was the same: inability to sustain shareholder value creation, which is the bottom-line meaning of value for publicly-held companies.

One reason sustained value creation is difficult is because of a phenomenon called 'value migration'. That is, over time, the value that an organization produces tends to diminish. Think, for example, of purchasing an automobile in 1965. If you got power steering, power brakes, and power windows in your car, you probably felt that you were getting special value. Certainly, these features were defined as exceeding the normal value contained in most automobiles. A price premium could also be charged by manufacturers for those features. Within a relatively short period of time, however, the price premium diminished, expectations of customers mandated that almost all cars had power steering, power brakes, and power windows, and no special value was associated with their presence. In fact, if these features were absent, most customers felt they were getting a less-than-valuable car. In other words, value had migrated away from these features. This phenomenon occurs in almost all products and services that eventually become commodities. Competitors develop the ability to copy the new features, produce them for a lower cost, and sell them to customers as standard products. The competitive advantage of the original value diminishes. This means, simply, that the challenge of creating value is never ending in organizations.

An important Compete quadrant change lever for organizations, therefore, is the capability to enhance their value creating competency. That is, the more sustained value the firm creates, the more competitive and successful it will be. Fortunately, creating sustained value is a deceptively simple proposition, yet it is obviously not universally practiced. If it were, all firms would survive, all organizations would flourish, and no enterprises would experience bankruptcy. The ability to create sustained economic value is the factor that separates winning companies from losing companies, survivors from casualties, and spectacular successes from also-rans. We discuss three simple keys to value creation here.

Clearly Define Value

Many organizations haven't yet defined what value creation means to them. Or they have so many definitions of value – many of which conflict in specific circumstances – that employees end up being confused about the core mission of the company. One manager's frustrated description of his firm illustrates this problem:

> Our company is run by an alphabet soup. We have EPS, ROE, RONA, ROI, Operating Profit, Customer Satisfaction Scores, Employee Satisfaction Scores, Stock Price, IRR, NPV, and payback, all affecting how we make decisions. At the end of the day I sometimes feel like screaming: 'What do you really want me to do here?' I don't think I'm the only one who's confused.

If value is defined in a bank, for example, as maximizing profit, loan officers will deny loans to, for example, developers of low-income housing or urban renewal projects because they are not likely to pay back big dividends. On the other hand, if value is defined in a bank as enhancing community development and improving the quality of life for city residents, the same loan application may be approved because it would likely create a great deal of value. Neither definition of value is necessarily superior, of course. This is not a question of one right answer. It is just that the organization must be very clear, both to their employees and to the shareholders, what their core definition of value is.

Understand the Key Value Drivers

Value drivers are the factors that affect or promote the creation of value. In a manufacturing plant, for example, key value drivers might include such things as the quality of training received by factory workers, the innate talent of the employees, the complexity of the manufacturing process, the design of the factory, and relationships with suppliers. These factors all affect the actual *production* of outcomes; they are not outcomes themselves. Outcomes include things like product quality, on-time delivery, and manufacturing cost per unit. These outcomes are affected by the value drivers, so that the leader of this manufacturing plant would be charged with managing the drivers that influence the outcomes. A common mistake is that managers often focus excessively on desired outcomes without paying attention to the key value drivers. They miss achieving their outcomes because they manage the wrong thing. It is the value drivers that give the company its competitive advantage.

The key value driver for Wal-Mart is asset turnover, and Wal-Mart's supplier relationships and logistical systems serve as the levers the company pulls to maximize asset turnover. General Electric's former CEO, Jack Welch, claimed that the intelligence of GE's employees along with a climate of constant learning were the key value drivers of that firm's success. When Ray Kroc purchased McDonalds from the McDonald brothers, he redefined the value drivers for that industry. Rather than focusing on selling franchises in order to increase profits (which had been the common strategy up to then), he focused on an alternative set of key value drivers in order to benefit franchise owners – such as simple menus with limited items to simplify restaurant management, franchisee training at McDonalds University, national advertising campaigns that benefited all McDonalds restaurants, super-clean restaurants, fast service with a smile, and so on. In other words, a focus on key value drivers allowed him to achieve desired outcomes that would not have been achieved had he focused only on the outcomes themselves.

Articulate the Competitive Strategy

A strategy is a roadmap for getting to a goal. Strategy determines how resources are to be allocated, both human and financial. It provides a mechanism by which an organization can examine all of its value-creating activities and decide which ones to focus on in order to reach its goals. Strategy is thus a way to achieve focus. One of the advantages of a clearly enunciated strategy is that it can help the organization cut out some activities – even if they are creating value – so as to concentrate more effectively on the key value drivers that maximize value. In other words, an important objective of strategy is to say no to good ideas. A good illustration of the power of strategy is the birth and explosive development of Starbucks, the global coffee powerhouse.

In 1987 the coffee industry in the United States was dominated by three major players, Procter & Gamble (P&G), General Foods, and Nestlé. Collectively these three giants accounted for 90 percent of the $8 billion retail market. By 1988, P&G was winning the market share battle with its Folgers brand, but profit margins were declining for all the major competitors, along with a decline in per-capita coffee consumption in the United States. This was a mature commodity business.

The major competitors all shared the same strategy which was to target the entire grocery-buying public and sell mass-produced ground coffee that was made with inexpensive Robusta beans and vacuum-packed for long shelf-life. The key dimension on which the major producers competed was price. None of the firms was creating much value.

In 1986, Howard Schultz opened the first Starbucks café in Seattle. By the end of 1994, Starbucks was a publicly traded company worth well over $1 billion. Starbucks had taken a mature commodity business and turned it into a lucrative, fast-growing business where market share was stolen from the big three competitors wholesale.

Schultz had a very different strategy. First, instead of targeting the entire grocery-buying public, he focused on upwardly mobile white-collar workers familiar with the European 'cappuccino culture.' This meant avoiding grocery store selling, and instead, opening cafes that were close to customers' places of work. Second, rather than competing on price, Starbucks decided to offer its customers the entire experience of having fine coffee in an inviting café atmosphere. This meant producing high quality coffee with more expensive Arabica beans and selling the product at relatively high profit margins. Starbucks' success can be attributed to a strategy that focused on a different set of value drivers than the big three competitors – quality instead of quantity, restaurants instead of grocery stores, close proximity as opposed to supermarket selling. In the end, this strategy created one of the most notable success stories in American business and created a new, growing industry out of an old, declining one.

As pointed out before, no firm can succeed in a spectacular way and over a long period of time without attending to each of the four quadrants. Starbucks illustrates this principle by also excelling in the Collaborate quadrant. Employees are provided continuous encouragement, feedback and recognition for their achievements. All employees who work more than 20 hours a week are given stock options and health-care benefits. There is formalized collaboration through teams and examples of successful performance are provided to employees. In the Control quadrant, Starbucks breaks down complex tasks into small and simple tasks that the employees in its cafés can master. Moreover, the necessary resources and information are provided and confidence is created through the continuous provision of high-quality service to customers and concern for employees. Starbucks' achievements in the Compete quadrant are no less impressive. Its revenues grew an average of 20 percent per year for the decade prior to 2003, and is stock price was up 56 percent during 2003, a stunning 3028 percent since its IPO. Finally Starbucks' founder, Howard Schultz seems to have a passion for the Create quadrant. He has articulated a vision of innovation and rapid growth for the company. To quote him, 'We're in the second inning of a nine-inning game. We are just beginning to tap into all sorts of new markets, customers and products.'

Of course, other keys to creating sustained economic value can be identified, but the three mentioned here which are based on the work of Thakor (2000) – clearly define value, understand the key value drivers, and articulate the competitive strategy – highlight very important ones. And,

COLLABORATE	CREATE
2. Make certain that everyone in the organization understands that the goal is to maximize value over the *long run*. People must be assigned to the task of teaching what value means to others in the firm. 3. All employees must be educated about what the key value drivers are. Identify which value drivers are under their control.	5. Create a strategy that positions the organization to compete in the future, including creating new value drivers not yet recognized by the competition.
CONTROL	COMPETE
1. Choose a clear definition of value for the organization. Maximizing shareholder value is often preferred in publicly-owned firms.	4. Tie reward and recognition systems (compensation) to the value drivers employees can control. Motivate employees to concentrate on key value drivers more than on desired outcomes.

Figure 8.6   Steps for creating sustained economic value

once again, the Competing Values Framework helps identify the well-roundedness that must be present in any change lever in any of the quadrants. Figure 8.6 summarizes the five steps in creating sustained economic value.

SUMMARY

In this chapter we have provided examples of change levers that have been especially effective in helping organizations improve in each of the four quadrants represented in the Competing Values Framework. Of course, many more levers – that is, a wide variety of tools and techniques used to drive change – are available in each quadrant. Effective leaders create value by identifying those that best fit their circumstances, but the Competing Values Framework helps them know how to approach that task. Explaining these four levers in detail, let alone discussing a large number of additional levers, requires more space then is available in this volume. Additional assistance can be found on the competing values website: competingvalues.com. What we intend here is simply to highlight two key principles. First, key change levers can be identified in each of the Competing Values Framework quadrants which have been proven effective in enhancing the value creation success of organizations. Second, implementing these change levers successfully requires that all four quadrants of the Competing Values Framework be considered.

9. Conclusions about the structure of value

In this book we have explained the Competing Values Framework as a value creation tool. The framework was originally developed in the scholarly organizational studies literature as a way to evaluate organizational effectiveness, organization culture, and individual leadership behavior. We have significantly extended the implications of the framework, however, to encompass various forms of value creation in organizations. The key insight of the Competing Values Framework is that value creation requires recognizing the inherent tensions that exist in different forms of value creation, and that focusing too little or too much in a particular value creation quadrant will impede effective value creation. It is quite common, however, for organizations to fall into the trap of either focusing inadequately or excessively on one quadrant at the expense of other quadrants. As shown in Figure 9.1, this leads to predictable problems.

Figure 9.1 suggests that an under-emphasis or ignoring any of the quadrants leads to disastrous consequences. On the other hand, an over-emphasis in any of the quadrants, especially at the exclusion of its opposite competing quadrant, also leads to negative outcomes. For example, ignoring relationships, human development, and teamwork in the Collaborate quadrant will lead, over time, to 'slow death' (Quinn, 1996), or the loss of commitment, engagement, and energy in a system. Employees become unattached and uncaring, and the organization dwindles. However, it is also possible to go overboard in emphasizing the Collaborate quadrant by, for example, excessive discussion where no conclusions or actions result, unproductive participation where non-invested people are given voice which merely sidetracks progress, emotional dominance where rational analysis is set aside in favor of emotional appeals or the transitory moods of the leader, or individualism where employees are overly-selfish and self-centered. In this case, the organization resembles an irresponsible country club where no progress is made aside from chumminess, self-congratulation, or comfort at the expense of improvement.

Similarly, ignoring the Create quadrant factors leads to stagnation with no new ideas or activities being created. An absence of learning and changing leads to languishing. An over-emphasis on the Create quadrant,

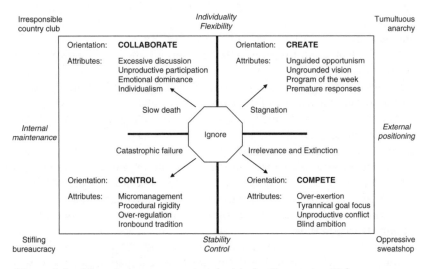

Figure 9.1   Negative zones associated with the Competing Values Framework

however, also produces harmful consequences. Unguided opportunism where every new opportunity is pursued, ungrounded vision that lacks substance and is more akin to dreaming and wild fantasy, introducing the program of the week where something new is constantly being launched or tried, and premature responses to opportunities or ideas rather than performing appropriate due-diligence all can lead to a tumultuous anarchy. The organization spins out of control by pursuing too much change.

Over and under-emphasizing the Compete quadrant also leads to negative consequences. Ignoring Compete factors – for example, not responding to customers, not achieving output goal, disregarding the competition – will obviously lead to irrelevance and eventual extinction. On the other hand, focusing too much on the Compete quadrant can produce the defensiveness and resistance associated with an oppressive sweatshop. For example, over-exertion and high levels of pressure to perform lead to feelings of burnout. A tyrannical goal focus can make important issues that are not directly related to the dogged pursuit of a goal irrelevant, such as the work environment, work–life balance, or setting aside resources for creating endeavors. Competitiveness frequently escalates into conflict, and an over-emphasis on winning can lead to unproductive conflict where resources are deflected in order to fight a battle rather than produce a desired result. Blind ambition, either on the part of the organization or its leaders, can also drive the organization down dangerous paths, as in 'become #1 or #2 in your market or else be sold.' This radical mandate by Jack Welch effectively shut down new product development and ventures into new arenas within General Electric for several years.

The Control quadrant is often the one that is described negatively in its extreme forms. No one trumpets bureaucracy. We have argued, however, that organizations cannot succeed without adequate emphasis in this quadrant. However, an absence of controls leads to catastrophic failure because of lack of accountability, inefficiency, and skyrocketing errors. On the other hand, micromanaging the workforce so that they have little discretion, procedural rigidity that drives out independent thinking, over-regulation where outside controls make it impossible to do anything but respond to rules, standards, or procedures, and iron-bound tradition and the 'not-invented-here syndrome' where barriers exist to any suggestions for change or improvement, all lead to a stifling bureaucracy. The organization remains frozen in time.

The key lesson, of course, is that both over- and under-emphasis in each quadrant, as well as ignoring the opposite or competing quadrant, will almost always lead to deteriorating performance over time and a lack of value creation. On the other hand, paradoxical organizations and leaders – those that pursue simultaneously contradictory strategies at the same time – are those that tend to succeed and that create value that far exceeds the norm.

In addition to this overall prescription, we also desire to summarize in a simple form several other leadership lessons associated with the Competing Values Framework. These are not meant to be comprehensive rules of thumb nor to be prescribed in every organization or for every improvement effort. They are, however, empirically grounded assertions and have been found to be lead most organizations toward highly successful performance and, particularly, to the creation of value.

A SUMMARY OF LEADERSHIP LESSONS FOR CREATING VALUE

We conclude the book with a brief summary of leadership lessons for value creation. These leadership lessons summarize the key points explained in the previous eight chapters.

Organizational tensions always exist. Competing values, preferences, and priorities exist in every organization. Effectively managing those tensions can create value and lead to extraordinarily high organizational effectiveness.

Personal tensions always exist. Competing values and their resulting tensions exist within every individual leader as well. Effective leadership and personal value creation depends on being aware of and managing those contradictory tensions.

The Competing Values Framework identifies key tensions. The Competing Values Framework serves as a sense-making map. It helps categorize, organize, and simplify complex phenomena. In particular, it highlights the competing demands that exist in all organizations and leaders.

The Competing Values Framework provides a theory of effective leadership and value creation through managing tensions. A theory about successful leadership, organizational performance, and value creation emerges from the Competing Values Framework. It includes predictions that congruence among disparate elements in organizations leads to success, paradoxical management is required for effectiveness, and comprehensive strategies and tactics representing all parts of the Competing Values Framework are needed to create value.

Two types of tensions are fundamental in organizations. The primary competing dimensions that must be managed in organizations are the trade-offs between, first, flexibility and dynamism in contrast to stability and control, and second, internal dynamics in contrast to external positioning.

Two secondary tensions exist in organizations. The secondary competing dimensions that must be managed relate to organizational change. They involve the trade-offs inherent in the *magnitude* of change – namely, transformational versus incremental change – and the trade-offs inherent in *velocity* of change – namely, fast versus developmental change.

Four quadrants summarize the fundamental and secondary competing values. The Competing Values Framework produces four quadrants – the Collaborate quadrant which is competing with the Compete quadrant, and the Create quadrant which is competing with the Control quadrant. The diagonal quadrants are opposites, representing the four major ways in which individuals organize information, structure organizations, display leadership competencies, develop core values and culture, and so on. The fundamental dimensions upon which the Competing Values Framework is based have been independently reproduced in a variety of disciplines.

Alignment across the quadrants leads to effective performance. For successful value creation, it is necessary to align different levels of analysis, namely, external outcomes, internal organizational activities, and individual leadership behaviors, so that each of the four quadrants is pursued at each level of analysis.

The Competing Values Framework encourages both/and thinking. Both/and thinking tends to create more mature, sophisticated, and value-creating leadership than either/or thinking as it relates to competing values. Both/and thinking requires more cognitive complexity and the ability to tolerate 'schizmogenesis' – or, holding contradictory thoughts in the mind at the same time. The Competing Values Framework organizes elements in such a way that both/and thinking is possible.

The Competing Values Framework encourages the creation of new leadership alternatives. The Competing Values Framework is useful for creating completely new approaches to leadership which, in turn, help to create new forms of value and positive deviance in organizations. That is, leaders can go beyond merely integrating opposing ideas to actually create a new set of leadership alternatives. This occurs by merging positive opposite concepts. For example, value creation can be produced by autonomous engagement (Compete and Collaborate quadrants), practical vision (Control and Create quadrants), teachable confidence (Create and Control quadrants), and caring confrontation (Collaborate and Compete quadrants).

Using the Competing Values Framework fosters value-adding and cost-reducing approaches. Value is created when the costs of producing something are less than the benefits provided by that thing. Value is depleted when costs outweigh benefits. The Competing Values Framework is a useful tool for identifying ways to create value – namely by finding ways to enhance value and reduce costs.

The Competing Values Framework helps map organizational culture. Virtually all organizations develop a dominant culture over time. Using the Competing Values Framework, those cultures can be clearly mapped and described.

Subculture congruence fosters effective performance. Different subunits within an organization tend to have different subcultures. However, a fundamental culture unique to the overall organization should be present in each subculture. Sub-cultural congruence leads to higher levels of effectiveness and value creation than incongruent subcultures.

Organizational cultures evolve predictably. Organizational cultures and the associated problems and issues evolve in a predictable pattern. Most new organizations are dominated by the Create quadrant, evolve into dominance by the Create and Collaborate quadrants, then transition into dominance in the Control quadrant, and finally become mature by emphasizing the Compete and Control quadrants. Without special attention being paid, many mature organizations become dominated by the two bottom quadrants in the framework and lose their ability to perform well in the Create and Collaborate quadrants.

Congruence of leadership competencies and organizational culture leads to effectiveness. To create value, managers' competencies must be congruent with their organization's dominant culture. Demonstrating leadership competencies in the quadrants that dominate the organization's culture is associated with higher levels of success for the leader.

Proficiency in competing competencies is required of leaders. To create value, organizations and leaders must possess at least average competency in all four quadrants of the framework. They do not acquire blind spots and major areas of weakness in any of the quadrants. This does not mean that they possess dominance and strength in each of the four quadrants, but they must have skills and capabilities to at least a moderate degree in each of the four quadrants.

The Competing Values Framework can predict financial success. Identifying proxy financial measures for each of the Competing Values Framework quadrants produces a much more comprehensive financial management approach than other alternatives such as the 'balanced score-card' or 'economic value added.' Pursuing financial strategies in all four quadrants leads to outperforming the market by a substantial margin.

The Competing Values Framework can help establish financial investment strategy. Using the Competing Values Framework to compare an organization's own financial performance with its industry averages can provide guidance regarding where the firm should invest in order to create the most value. Empirical analyses have identified the extent to which shareholder value can be enhanced by focusing on and investing in particular areas of financial weakness based on a competing values financial performance profile.

The Competing Values Framework can help establish a comprehensive measurement system. Objective measures in each of the four quadrants – for example, financial measures, outcome measures, process measures, capability measures – should be assessed in every organization. The organization's strategies can then support and sustain those objective measures. Unfortunately, most organizations do a better job in identifying hard measures in the bottom two quadrants – Control and Compete – than they do in the top two quadrants – Collaborate and Create.

A package of competing values assessment instruments help align key elements of leadership and organizations. A variety of assessment instruments based on the Competing Values Framework are available. The advantage of having a package of instruments all based on the same framework is that a common language is enabled in the organization, goals and strategies can be aligned, values and leadership competencies can be integrated, successful performance markedly enhanced, and value created. Currently available instruments assess leadership competencies, organizational culture, performance outcomes, organizational change strategies, and personal orientation.

Personal leadership competency in the Competing Values Framework is associated with success. Individual leadership competency in each one of the four quadrants is associated with significantly higher personal performance and organizational performance. High personal competency does not, unfortunately, predict individual salary increases or financial remuneration. That is, significant value is created for the organization, but most firms' remuneration systems seem not to reward personal competency.

The Competing Values Framework can help diagnose and change organizational culture. Because organizational culture is a major predictor of whether or not attempted organizational changes actually succeed, it is an important element for leaders to manage. An assessment instrument as well as a proven process for changing organizational culture has been widely applied and is available from the authors. This culture change process can help provide a rational way to approach what is often an intractable issue in many firms.

The Competing Values Framework can predict the success of mergers and acquisitions. The success or failure of mergers and acquisitions can be predicted with at least 90 percent accuracy just on the basis of cultural congruence. That is, when the cultures of two merging firms are congruent, the probability of success is high. When they possess incompatible cultures, the probability of success is low. This result holds regardless of industry or size of the organizations.

Numerous tools based on the Competing Values Framework can enhance the creation of value in organizations. A variety of tools and techniques are available to enhance value creation and high performance in each of the four quadrants of the Competing Values Framework. In the Collaborate quadrant, empirical evidence suggests that empowering the workforce by fostering self-efficacy, self-determination, personal consequence, meaningfulness, and trust leads to significantly higher value creation. In the Control quadrant, value creation in enhanced through process assessment, process analysis, and process redesign, enacted particularly through a focus on customers, boundarylessness, uncovering root causes, and leanness. In the Create quadrant value creation is enhanced through innovation-fostering processes. For example, pulling people apart and putting people together, monitoring and implementing sharp-pointed prods, and rewarding multiple roles – including idea champions, sponsors, and orchestrators – are among the key strategies for enabling value creation. In the Compete quadrant, value creation is enhanced by managing and compensating for value migration, primarily through clearly defining what is meant by value, understanding the key value drivers, and articulating clearly the competitive strategies.

ADDITIONAL RESOURCES

In addition to these leadership lessons, a variety of other sources are available for learning about the applicability of the Competing Values Framework and value creation. For example, DeGraff and colleagues have used the Competing Values Framework to explain the innovation process, see: Jeff DeGraff, and Katherine Lawrence (2001), *Creativity at Work*, San Francisco: Jossey-Bass; as well as Jeff DeGraff and Shawn Quinn (2006), *The Innovation Genome*, New York: McGraw Hill.

The process of diagnosing and changing organizational culture was addressed by Kim Cameron and Robert Quinn (2006), see: Cameron, Kim S. and Robert E. Quinn (2005), *Diagnosing and Changing Organizational Culture*, San Francisco: Jossey-Bass.

Developing management competencies was discussed in a book by Robert Quinn (1988), *Beyond Rational Management*, San Francisco: Jossey-Bass.

The topic of value and the creation of value was address by Anjan Thakor (2000), *Becoming a Better Value Creator*, San Francisco: Jossey-Bass.

The use of the Competing Values Framework to diagnose extraordinary organizational success and positively deviant performance was written by Kim Cameron and Marc Lavine (2006), *Making the Impossible Possible*, San Francisco: Berrett Koehler.

In addition to these written resources, other aids are available from: competingvalues.com.

References

Bandura, A. (1997), *Self-Efficacy: The Exercise of Control*, New York: W.H. Freeman.

Bass, B.M. and R.M. Stogdill (1990), *Bass and Stogdill's Handbook of Leadership*, New York: Free Press.

Bateson, G. (2002), *Mind and Nature: A Necessary Unity (Advances in Systems Theory, Complexity and the Human Sciences)*, Boston: Hampton Press.

Boquist, J.A., T.T. Milbourn and A.V. Thakor (2000), *The Value Sphere*, Bloomington, IN: Value Integration Associates.

Cameron, K.S. (1980), 'Critical questions in assessing organization effectiveness,' *Organizational Dynamics*, **9**, 66–80.

Cameron, K.S. (1998), 'Strategic organizational downsizing: an extreme case,' *Research in Organizational Behavior*, **20**, 185–229.

Cameron, K.S. (2005a), 'Solving problems creatively and analytically,' in D.A. Whetten and K.S. Cameron (eds), *Developing Management Skills*, Upper Saddle River, NJ: Prentice Hall, pp. 153–205.

Cameron, K.S. (2005b), 'Empowering and delegating,' in D.A. Whetten and K.S. Cameron (eds), *Developing Management Skills*, Upper Saddle River, NJ: Prentice Hall, pp. 397–442.

Cameron, K.S. (2005c), 'The critical role of management skills,' in D.A. Whetten and K.S. Cameron (eds), *Developing Management Skills*, Upper Saddle River, NJ: Prentice Hall, pp. 1–22.

Cameron, K.S. (2006), 'Good and not bad: standards for high performance amidst change,' *Academy of Management Learning and Education Journal*.

Cameron, K.S. and C. Mora (2002), 'Corporate culture and financial success of mergers and acquisitions,' working paper, Ross School of Business, University of Michigan.

Cameron, K.S. and M. Lavine (2006), *Making the Impossible Possible: Leading Extraordinary Performance – The Rocky Flats Story*, San Francisco: Berrett Koehler.

Cameron, K.S. and R.E. Quinn (2006), *Diagnosing and Changing Organizational Culture: Based on the Competing Values Framework*, San Francisco: Jossey-Bass.

Cameron, K.S., M.U. Kim and D.A. Whetten (1987a), 'Organizational effects of decline and turbulence,' *Administrative Science Quarterly*, **32**, 222–40.

Cameron, K.S., D.A. Whetten and M.U. Kim (1987b), 'Organizational dysfunctions of decline,' *Academy of Management Journal*, **30**, 126–38.

Collins, J.C. (2000), *Good to Great*, New York: Harper Collins.

Collins, J.C. and J.I. Porras (1994), *Built to Last*, New York: Harper Collins.

DeGraff, J. and K.A. Lawrence (2002), *Creativity at Work*, San Francisco: Jossey-Bass.

Dutton, J.E. (2003), *Energize Your Workplace*, San Francisco: Jossey-Bass.

Dutton, Jane E., Peter J. Frost, Monica C. Worline, Jacoba M. Lilius and Jason M. Kanov (2002), 'Leading in times of trauma,' *Harvard Business Review*, January, 54–61.

Emerson, R.W. (1996), 'Goethe; or, the writer, representative men' (1850), in *The Columbia World of Quotations*, quotation 20146, accessed at www.bortleby.com/66/46/20146.html.

Fortune (2003), 'Who's afraid of a new product? Not W.L. Gore. It has mastered the art of storming completely different businesses,' *Fortune*, 10 November 2003, 78–86.

Friedman, M. (1996), *Type A Behavior: Its Diagnosis and Treatment*, New York: Kluwer Academic Publishers.

Gadiesh, O. and J.L. Gilbert (1998), '*How to Map Your Industry's Profit Pool*,' Boston, MA: Harvard Business School Press.

Gordon, A. (1959), 'The turn of the tide,' *Readers Digest*, 43–5.

Lawrence, P.R. and J.W. Lorsch (1967), *Organizations and Environment*, Homewood, IL: Irwin.

Lawrence, P.R. and N. Nohria (2002), *Driven: How Human Nature Shapes Our Choices*, San Francisco: Jossey-Bass.

Liker, J.K. (2005), *The Toyota Way*, New York: McGraw Hill.

Mishra, A.K. (1992), 'Organizational response to crisis,' unpublished doctoral dissertation, University of Michigan.

Quinn, Robert E. (1988), *Beyond Rational Management*, San Francisco: Jossey-Bass.

Quinn, R.E. (1996), *Deep Change or Slow Death*, San Francisco: Jossey-Bass.

Quinn, R.E. (2003), *Change the World*, San Francisco: Jossey-Bass.

Quinn, R.E. and K.S. Cameron (1983), 'Organizational life cycles and shifting criteria of effectiveness: some preliminary evidence,' *Management Science*, **29**, 33–51.

Quinn, Robert E. and John Rohrbaugh (1983), 'A spacial model of effectiveness criteria: towards a competing values approach to organizational analysis,' *Management Science*, **29**, 363–77.

Quinn, R.E. and G.M. Spreitzer (1997), 'The road to empowerment: seven questions every leader should consider,' *Organizational Dynamics*, **25**, 37–49.

Rothenberg, A. (1979), *The Emerging Goddess*, Chicago: University of Chicago Press.

Spreitzer, G.M. (1992), 'When organizations dare,' unpublished doctoral dissertation, Ross School of Business, University of Michigan.

ten Have, S., W. Ten Have, A.F. Stevens, M. Vander Elst and F. Pol-Coyne (2003), *Key Management Models: The Management Tools and Practices that will Improve Your Business*, London: Prentice-Hall.

Thakor, A.V. (2000), *Becoming a Better Value Creator*, San Francisco: Jossey-Bass.

Tichy, N.M. and S. Sherman (2001), *Control Your Destiny or Someone Else Will*, New York: HarperCollins.

Torbert, W.R. (1987), *Managing the Corporate Dream*, Homewood, IL: Dow Jones–Irwin.

Warner, C.T. (2001), *Bonds That Make Us Free*, Provo, UT: Shadow Mountain Press.

Whetten, D.A. and K.S. Cameron (2005), *Developing Management Skills*, 6th edn, Upper Saddle River, NJ: Prentice Hall.

Wilber, K. (2001), *A Theory of Everything: An Integral Vision of Business, Politics, Science and Spirituality*, Boston: Shambhala Books.

Index